"Tara Banks' words and revelations have shaped who I am today. And to this day, I'm still finding everyday fruit, sown from the seeds of Tara's most influential, inspiring, and empowering words spoken into my own life. If planted and tended to, I know these words will produce much fruit in your life, the same as mine."

—**Brandon Lake,** Multi-Grammy Award-winning Christian Artist

"The wisdom in these pages will transform your heart and life. With clarity, warmth, and a deep grounding in Scripture, Tara lovingly guides you to cultivate the fruit of the Spirit in every season of life. This book is an invitation to grow, reflect, and walk in the fullness of all that God has for you. I encourage you to take your time, lean in, and allow the Holy Spirit to work through Tara's insights, bringing lasting change and causing you to flourish."

—**Andi Andrew,** author, *She Is free, Fake or Follower, Friendship-It's Complicated, Braving Change,* speaker, and host of *Coffee with Andi* podcast

"*Finding Everyday Fruit* by Tara L. Banks is a powerful and practical guide to living out the fruit of the Spirit in daily life. Having known and worked with Tara for over 25 years, I can attest that she not only writes about these principles, but fully embodies them. This book is a must-read for anyone seeking genuine spiritual growth and transformation."

—**Greg Surratt,** Founding Pastor, Seacoast Church, Charleston, SC

FINDING EVERYDAY FRUIT

Discover and Develop a Life
Formed by the Fruit of the Spirit

Tara L. Banks

Cover & interior design by Typewriter Creative Co.
Edited by Marney McNall
Floral design by Lydia Banks
Watercolor images by Anna Zaharchenrko and Lydia Banks
Author bio photo by Ellen Everson @ellencharisphoto

ISBN 979-8-9874704-5-9 (Paperback)
ISBN 979-8-9874704-4-2 (Hardcover)
ISBN 979-8-9874704-7-3 (eBook)

For Ethan, Lydia, and Brody—the joy you bring to my life is more than all the sand in Hanalei Bay.

But the fruit of the Spirit is love, joy, peace, patience, kindness, goodness, faithfulness, gentleness, self-control; against such things there is no law.

Galatians 5:22-23 (ESV)

"God spoke today in flowers and I who was waiting on words almost missed the conversation."[1]

Ingrid Goff-Maidoff

CONTENTS

INTRODUCTION 9

01: LOVE 14
Part 01: Finding the Fruit of LOVE in the Word of God
    Judas' Betrayal 21

Part 02: Finding the Fruit of LOVE in the World
    Elderberry Syrup 27
    Counting 30

02: JOY 34
Part 01: Finding the Fruit of JOY in the Word of God
    Mary Magdalene at the Tomb 39

Part 02: Finding the Fruit of JOY in the World
    The Dryer 45
    The Jeep 48

03: PEACE 52
Part 01: Finding the Fruit of PEACE in the Word of God
    Jesus Calming the Storm 57

Part 02: Finding the Fruit of PEACE in the World
    The Fig Tree 63
    Perspective 66

04: PATIENCE 70
Part 01: Finding the Fruit of PATIENCE in the Word of God
    Peter's Denial 75

Part 02: Finding the Fruit of PATIENCE in the World
    The Journey 83
    The Bowl of Chili 86

05: KINDNESS 90
Part 01: Finding the Fruit of KINDNESS in the Word of God
    The Samaritan Woman 95

Part 02: Finding the Fruit of KINDNESS in the World
    The Umbrella 103
    The Airplane Row 106

06: GOODNESS   112

Part 01: Finding the Fruit of GOODNESS in the Word of God
    Moses on the Mountain   117

Part 02: Finding the Fruit of GOODNESS in the World
    Banned Words   123
    Good Grief   127

07: FAITHFULNESS   130

Part 01: Finding the Fruit of FAITHFULNESS in the Word of God
    Daniel and the Den of Lions   135

Part 02: Finding the Fruit of FAITHFULNESS in the World
    Equilibrium   141
    The Tides   145

08: GENTLENESS   148

Part 01: Finding the Fruit of GENTLENESS in the Word of God
    Casting the First Stone   153

Part 02: Finding the Fruit of GENTLENESS in the World
    Tongue and Tone   159
    Training Wheels   163

09: SELF-CONTROL   168

Part 01: Finding the Fruit of SELF-CONTROL in the Word of God
    Jesus on the Cross   173

Part 02: Finding the Fruit of SELF-CONTROL in the World
    Fold Your Hands   177
    See Green   181

CONCLUSION   185

ACKNOWLEDGMENTS   192

LEARN HAWAIIAN   194

THE MEANING OF "ALOHA"   196

NOTES   198

ABOUT THE AUTHOR   200

INTRODUCTION

With every sun's rising, surprise us with Your love, satisfy us with Your kindness. Then we will sing with joy and celebrate every day we are alive.

Psalm 90:14 (VOICE)

I've often heard pastors jokingly say that they are hesitant to give sermons about certain topics because they know the Lord will require them to live out what they are teaching during the week. It is much like that when writing a book about the fruit of the Spirit. I knew full well that as I stepped out in faith to write about how to discover and develop a life formed by the fruit of the Spirit, I was going to be challenged to live it out.

And I was right.

Almost instantly, I found myself faced with how my attitudes and actions reflected—or not—each fruit of the Spirit. Love was tested in how I chose to respond to my husband. I allowed my circumstances to dictate my emotions, taking me far from joy and peace. I reacted impatiently, was not gentle or kind in my speech, and failed in my efforts to live a life filled with goodness. Too often, I didn't come through for people I love, showing a lack of faithfulness in my commitment to them. My mind was out of control, racing with thoughts that were keeping me from seeing, much less developing a life that looked more like the one Jesus lived. And most days, all of that was happening before 9:00 AM. (Anyone else?)

Then, just as I was knee-deep in editing and within weeks of turning in my manuscript, in a freak accident on my front porch, I got a severe concussion that essentially shut down my life for months. I had a hard time focusing, let alone reading or writing. (Do you know how hard it is to write a book when you can't look at a computer screen?) Yes, I was learning in real time how to be patient and gentle with myself while right in the middle of writing a book about those very things. Talk about being challenged to live it out!

This writing-about-the-fruit-of-the-Spirit thing was certainly an adventure. *Fair warning: reading about it will be, too.*

But, if you're ready to dig deep and discover how to raise your awareness of the work of the Lord in your daily life and develop the fruit of the Spirit, this book is for you.

WHERE'S THE ACTUAL FRUIT?

I have a deep love for the Hawaiian Islands, so I chose tropical flowers and a corresponding color to represent each fruit of the Spirit instead of an actual piece of fruit...because, well, it's my book, and I can do what I want. So, if you were expecting to see fruit images in a book about the fruit of the Spirit, I'm sorry, but you'll be disappointed. However, the very talented Lydia Banks designed these florals for me, and I promise you won't miss the fruit. Each time you see a new floral icon or color throughout the book, I hope it serves as a visual reminder to reflect on how you can learn to develop that fruit of the Spirit and allow the simple things to show you the way to Jesus' heart. (Bonus: You might even learn a few Hawaiian words along the way.)

Each chapter has two parts. Part 01 introduces a fruit of the Spirit and retells a familiar Bible story showing that fruit in action. Part 02 shares practical examples of that fruit on display in the world around us.

THE BEST PLACE TO START GROWING FRUIT

There is no better place to start growing fruit—reflecting the nature and character of Jesus—than at the beginning, hand in hand with Him. If you are just curious about all of this and are picking up this book because the cover was lovely but still have lots of questions, I'm so glad you're here. It's okay to have questions, ask them, and seek Jesus at the same time. If you don't know Jesus and want to, we can make that happen right now! It is as simple as saying a beautiful little prayer that goes something like this:

Dear God,

I am grateful for Your love and presence in my life. I acknowledge that I am unable to forgive my own sins or earn my way to Heaven, so I place my trust in Jesus, who died on the cross, to bear my sins and make it possible for me to stand in Your holy presence. I believe in His resurrection and that He has done all that is necessary for me to be saved. With all my heart, and as best as I can, I transfer my trust to Jesus. Despite my many sins and failures, I am thankful that He has promised to walk with me, even with all my questions, and never leave me. I believe my life is different, starting today.

Amen.

If you just prayed that prayer, all of Heaven is rejoicing! There is no more significant decision you could make than to follow Jesus. He will never let you down. I'm celebrating YOU!

Whether you've just met Him or have been walking with Him your entire life, you are in the right place. Jesus is for us all.

SO HERE WE GO!

Grab your Bible, open your eyes, and be prepared to experience God's Spirit through His Word and this beautiful world He created.

With you, finding everyday fruit,

Java

Chapter 01

love

LOVE | KE ALOHA

As a child, I had my first real encounter with the Lord while visiting Hawaii. It was the first time I remember hearing His voice, although I would not be able to articulate it as such until many years later. As I left the island, my nose pressed against the airplane window, I watched, tears streaming down my 7-year-old face, as the tropical landscape gradually receded to a dot in the vast blue ocean and the island was out of sight.

I didn't want to go home—who would? But, it was more than that. In a way I couldn't understand at such an early age, and in a manner I still cannot fully explain, the Lord planted Hawaii in my heart. Looking out that airplane window, I heard Him in my Spirit as clearly as I've ever heard a voice say, "I'll always bring you back."

Even now, the memory of that moment brings tears to my eyes. Over the last 30 years, the Lord has been so faithful and gracious to allow me to visit many times. In His overwhelming kindness, He even allowed me to write most of this book while there in early 2024. One day, I hope to grow deep roots on that little dot of green in the middle of the ocean and be surrounded by all those beautiful tropical flowers, but for now, I trust Him to be faithful and always bring me back to my tiny Hawaii island "home." Every single time he does, He has taught me more about who He is and how to attend to those Spirit-laden seeds that He wants to cultivate in my life and help bloom. And, because He is a personal God and knows all my favorite things, He loves to use all of His creation, in particular, the flowers and colors of the islands, to teach me lessons about what the fruit of the Spirit looks like in His life and how to try to mirror it in mine.

So now, when I think about the fruit of the Spirit, I envision a huge bouquet of brightly colored tropical flowers, where each flower represents a different fruit of the Spirit and complements the others. In my imagination, as I learn to grow in the individual characteristics of His Spirit, it's as if that particular flower blooms all the more beautifully in the bouquet of my life.

When I considered what flower should represent love, the first fruit of the Spirit listed in Galatians 5:22-23, I knew it had to be a plumeria.

Let me tell you a little story.

Many years ago, I brought a plumeria plant home from Hawaii. It lived by my front door, and as it bloomed, it reminded me every day of my love for the islands. The delicate, fragrant flowers felt like such a gift from the Lord.

After years of enjoying it, watching it grow, and babying it in the un-Hawaiian winter weather we sometimes have in the South, it suddenly contracted a disease that would assuredly mark the end of its life. In a last-ditch effort to save it, I had no choice but to prune it severely and hold out hope for the best.

Several months later, and just when I was certain the disease and the severe pruning had killed it, that iron-will plumeria sprouted leaves and began looking even healthier than before! The Lord reminded me that sometimes, the deepest pruning in our lives can lead to the most significant growth.

Love is like that. To bloom and grow in love, we often have to begin by pruning things from our lives that will keep us from loving. Through this plumeria plant, the Lord began to teach me how to hear His voice. I think it's incredible that the Lord would be so loving and personal to use something I found so beautiful to help me experience His presence. If we pay attention, everything He's created can point to His great love for us and be used to show us how to be more like Him—even a plumeria.

The order of the fruit of the Spirit list is important. Love is first because it's the place to start a life filled and formed by God's Spirit. Everything else flows from that. If we want to grow in spiritual maturity, we have to first start with love. To grow in love means we have to be connected to Jesus, the source of it. To drive home this imagery, Jesus even called Himself "The Vine" (John 15:5). We, "the branches," receive the benefit of being grafted to Him. Over time, just like we see in creation, we bear the fruit of what The Vine produces in us. We grow. New things happen in us. This is the evidence that we've been with Him and are filled with His Spirit. Then, and only then, we have the capacity to grow in all of the other fruit of the Spirit. In the same way, green is the color of something fresh, of starting over, and it reminds me of that new growth. And since we're just getting started and learning to grow, green seems like the perfect color to choose here at the start to remind us of the fruit of love.

Delightfully loved ones, if he loved us with such tremendous love, then "loving one another" should be our way of life!

1 John 4:11 (TPT)

love

Let all that you do be done in love.
1 Corinthians 16:14 (ESV)

PART 01: FINDING THE FRUIT OF LOVE IN THE WORD OF GOD
-Judas' Betrayal-

"YOUR LOVE FOR ONE ANOTHER WILL PROVE TO THE WORLD THAT YOU ARE MY DISCIPLES." —JOHN 13:35 (NLT)

Jesus looked Judas in the eye, letting him know, *He knew.*

Moments later, the large wooden door shut, and the reverberations filled the room. It was the sound of selling out. Dust sparkled in the dim light of the oil lamp on the low table, and the room fell silent. Eleven sets of eyes scanned each other, catching glances, darting to Jesus, not knowing who should speak first or what to do next. The twelfth, Judas, had just walked out into the night after choosing disloyalty to Jesus and swallowing the bread of his betrayal. Finally, Jesus' voice broke into the quiet with a statement as bold as the way He broke into another silent night 33 years earlier:

> "So I give you a new command: Love each other deeply and fully. Remember the ways that I have loved you, and demonstrate your love for others in those same ways. Everyone will know you as My followers if you demonstrate your love to others." John 13:34-35 (VOICE)

Can you imagine that moment? After all that had just transpired, Jesus turned to the faithful disciples still reclining at the table, and told them that if they love, the world would know.

If we love...

When faced with a choice, we often don't choose to show the world what following Jesus looks like. We choose not to love. We choose the easy way out, or expect someone else will be loving. Or, if we're honest, we choose whatever makes us look good.

Jesus was reminding them (and us) that love is a choice. We don't have to love, but when we do, it informs the world what the fruit of the Spirit looks like and marks us inside and out as His.

Colossians 3:14 reminds us to "put on love." Which means it's an action; something we have to choose to do. This decision can change us and how we relate to the world and the people in it.

What we put on, or clothe ourselves in, not only protects us physically, but can also be used to identify or define us. Think about clothing for different types of weather. If it's cold outside, that outfit keeps you warm. If it's hot outside, it helps you stay cool. Your outfit doesn't change the weather but allows you to better acclimate to it.

"Putting on love" is no different. It doesn't change what's happening around us, but it allows us to experience life differently and can impact how we interact with the world around us.

So, what is love?

1 Corinthians 13, often dubbed "the love chapter," explains what love is. While each fruit of the Spirit is essential to a

well-rounded life and one that honors the Lord, love is the foundation for them all.

> If I could speak all the languages of earth and of angels, but didn't love others, I would only be a noisy gong or a clanging cymbal. If I had the gift of prophecy, and if I understood all of God's secret plans and possessed all knowledge, and if I had such faith that I could move mountains, but didn't love others, I would be nothing. If I gave everything I have to the poor and even sacrificed my body, I could boast about it; but if I didn't love others, I would have gained nothing. Love is patient and kind. Love is not jealous or boastful or proud or rude. It does not demand its own way. It is not irritable, and it keeps no record of being wronged. It does not rejoice about injustice but rejoices whenever the truth wins out. Love never gives up, never loses faith, is always hopeful, and endures through every circumstance. Three things will last forever—faith, hope, and love—and the greatest of these is love. 1 Corinthians 13:1–7, 13 (NLT)

Love is the root of all the fruit.

Without love, the believer is nothing. It has to be the absolute core from which we operate and draw the ability to embody all other attributes, or fruit, of His nature and character.

Jesus wanted to ensure the disciples knew that it was essential to continually seek out love. It would be the fruit that would most mark their ministry, mission, and meaning. If they couldn't get love right, the rest wouldn't matter. While gentleness, peace, or any other Spirit-markers are essential, love is noted as the singular identity for being a follower of Jesus. Love has to be first. This is why the order of the fruit of the Spirit listed in Galatians 5:22-23 matters.

As I read the biblical account of the bread-dipping scene with Judas and his dramatic exit, where he chose deception over devotion, my imagination runs wild. I envision Jesus comically pointing to the door that Judas just went through and saying something sarcastic about how loving people can be risky. (I'm so glad He didn't.) Instead, as Judas leaves, Jesus speaks to the disciples, and without *directly* mentioning the Judas-departure-elephant-in-the-room (but addressing it entirely in the way only Jesus could), He says, "So I give to you a new command: Love each other deeply and fully." (John 13:34 VOICE).

I'm sure you could have heard a pin drop.

Instead of being angry at Judas, Jesus is showing the disciples how to live out those very words in a situation unfolding right before their eyes. A messy one. A hard one. Talk about an object lesson.

Jesus was telling them not only to love God and others[2] but to "do" love—a new command. To love each other deeply. To live in a way that mirrors the way Jesus loved people. To choose to put on love when people are unlovable. To make a point to go out of your way to love when it isn't convenient and be willing to lay down your life for your friends—all in the name of love.

Jesus boldly declared the greatest commandment is to love. He could have said to live a good life, be kind to others, or make sure to call your mother. However, of everything He could have chosen, He chose love. Clearly, Jesus didn't select love because it's the easiest to emulate—it's likely the hardest. But He would never ask it of us if He weren't willing to be the first and best example. It's no wonder love was placed first as a fruit of a Spirit-filled life. This was consistent with His love-is-first heart and the sole motivation of "Operation: Rescue Humanity."

Jesus was following in the footsteps of His Father by showing that love was not just lived out in words, but also in deeds. The Father loved the world so much that He gave His son, Jesus, to save it (John 3:16). Jesus, in return, took on flesh and accepted "Operation: Rescue Humanity" as He gave Himself up as a love-ransom for us all (Matthew 20:28).

He was sent from Love, to be love, to teach us to love.

Through that complete work, Jesus showed the world the result of His once-and-for-all decision to put love into action and gave us an example to follow.

Jesus went first and showed us the way to love.

That evening, Jesus continued to teach the remaining disciples a lesson in love and made it clear that love would always be costly. Little did they know, Jesus was preparing to embody love and showcase it in a radical way like nothing the world had ever seen.

"My command is this: Love each other as I have loved you. Greater love has no one than this: to lay down one's life for one's friends." John 15:12–13 (NIV)

Even as He foreshadows His own death, the somber words are robed in love. Not only does He give the disciples this new commandment, to "do" love, but He is about to show them how to live it—even in death.

From the beginning of time, from that moment to this one, His focus has been and always will be love.

As modern-day disciples or apprentices to Jesus, we have also been given the commandment to choose love and be love, to let that be our calling card as we interact with those around us. Love is hard and costly and requires us to engage all the other fruit of the Spirit to live it out. Even so, Jesus has equipped us in our commission to love deeply and show the world what love looks like through the power of His Spirit working in us.

> "You didn't choose me, but I've chosen and commissioned you to go into the world to bear fruit. And your fruit will last, because whatever you ask of my Father, for my sake, he will give it to you! So this is my parting command: Love one another deeply!" John 15:16–17 (TPT)

Love is central to the life of every believer. Therefore, we should experience, receive, and live out lives of love in a way that sets us apart. As people who are filled with God's Spirit, let's not only be examples of that love, but also actively give it to others, and point them to the heart of Jesus, who is Love Himself.

PART 02: FINDING THE FRUIT OF LOVE IN THE WORLD
-Elderberry Syrup-

DELIGHTFULLY LOVED ONES, IF HE LOVED US WITH SUCH TREMENDOUS LOVE, THEN "LOVING ONE ANOTHER" SHOULD BE OUR WAY OF LIFE! —1 JOHN 4:11 (TPT)

Every fall and winter, it seems everyone gets sick. Everyone is coughing and sneezing and carrying on. (God bless the whole world and pass the tissues.) Not to be outdone, I usually join in at least once a year. This past year, when it was my turn, I caught a pretty bad cold, and when it was over, I thought, *Oh good. I've done it, and now I'll be super-immune to whatever might come my way.* Wrong.

A month later, I woke up feeling like I'd been hit by a truck. Not that any of us have time to be sick, but I was preparing to speak at a conference, had worship leading responsibilities at my church, and was working to get my small business off the ground—plus writing this book. So, being confined to the bed with exhaustion wasn't something that fit my schedule.

Mid-cold, my 17-year-old son came into my room and put a small bottle of elderberry syrup on the table.

"I was thinking about you today and thought this might help," he said quietly.

He's a thoughtful kid by nature. However, his thoughtfulness took an extra action step that day. You see, he had slept through his alarm, causing him to leave for work about 10 minutes later than he wanted. That delay put him behind on his morning duties at work and the rest of his already fully scheduled day. He knew he would need to balance going to work, getting to school, and then managing after-school activities. Even though his day was packed, he still decided to take the time to stop and get elderberry syrup for me.

He chose love. He chose to put aside his own agenda and put on inconvenience. He chose to see someone else's needs and go out of his way to do something about it. This is the fruit of love. This is clothing yourself with love (Colossians 3:14).

It's safe to say that even on our busiest and most stressful days, none of us carry even a fraction of the weight that Jesus carried while on Earth. Jesus was constantly going somewhere, constantly being needed, and constantly being interrupted. However, He was never fazed by the change of plans. He knew that even though He was on the most important rescue mission of all time, nothing was more important than displaying love to those around Him and becoming the primary example of love through each situation.

The interruption was the mission, not the distraction.

For Jesus, love was the primary motivation behind all He did. His actions were driven by love, and His motives were shaped by love. Out of the overflow of the love in His heart, He lived love in every conversation, touch, gesture, and smile.

When the fruit of the Spirit of love is in us, it will naturally come out in our actions. Those around us will not be able to help but taste the fruit of it in our lives. It will show up in thoughtful words, intentional actions, and selfless displays of putting others first. With His help, we can reflect the nature and character of Jesus in our lives and exhibit the evidence of the fruit He's developing in us as we try to live love like He does.

It might have just been a bottle of elderberry syrup, but to me, it was the fruit of love.

-Counting-

YOU HAVE KEPT RECORD OF MY DAYS OF WANDERING.
YOU HAVE STORED MY TEARS IN YOUR BOTTLE AND
COUNTED EACH OF THEM. —PSALM 56:8 (CEV)

I'm a professional musician, so I have to be good at counting. It helps me stay in time when I sing and helps me know when to stop singing or how long to hold out a note. Music is divided into measures, and those measures have counts. To get the song right, you have to count. I don't do it consciously anymore; it is just something that's *in* me.

Counting is also imperative in dance to stay in step with your partner, match the music, or appear as if you have rhythm. (Some of y'all need to learn to count.) While I certainly don't call myself a "dancer," I do know that while professional dancers don't consciously spend their life counting to eight, you can bet they know what count they are on at any given moment, in any given routine. It's just *in* them.

In my personal and professional life, I wear a lot of hats, and one of my favorites is being my family's Chief Household Operations Manager. Recently, I was busy around my house doing the CHOM things we do as wives and mothers, and I realized that I was unconsciously counting my steps. Not because I was trying to hit some exercise goal or because I had some wild desire to do math; I was just doing my little life. I tuned into the cadence happening in my mind. My brain was saying, *18, 19, 20...* as I walked.

I stopped dead in my tracks. *What in the world was I counting?* I stood there in silence, blinking. Listening. No music was on, so it wasn't coming from a song. I wasn't dancing (although I am known to bust a move at any given moment). My subconscious was busy counting something, and I didn't even know what it was or when it had started.

Where was the 1? When did it start?

I was on the second flight of stairs in my house, so I turned around and counted from the top. Sure enough, I was on #20.

My brain and body were counting steps, and I didn't even know it.

At that moment, I felt the Lord say to me, "I've been counting your steps and orchestrating your life—without you even knowing it—since before you were born. I've watched every step, been with you in every moment, and picked you up at every stumble. I've counted every hair on your head and know when you get them colored. I've kept a record of your tears and counted every single one. I know the number of times you've been wronged and the number of times you've wronged others (although I don't hold that against you). I've counted the nights of quiet prayers, the days of all-out war-worship, and the moments when you were sure you couldn't go on. I've counted them all."[3]

The fruit of His love that day looked like drawing my awareness to His purposeful and intentional affection toward me.

Without me knowing it, much like that unconscious counting I was doing, the Lord has been "counting" everything about me. His eyes have always been on me. His heart has always been for me. He has been with me. And even when I didn't think He did, He saw me. He has never left my side, even in the struggle. His love has been all around me, even when I wasn't aware.

It's part of His nature to see and fully know me. Even His name, El Roi, as declared by Hagar in Genesis 16:13, means "The God who sees me." No matter what I am going through, His loving gaze is always set on me. He gets me, and loves me anyway.

The more we recognize His love and acknowledge it in the simple acts of our day, the more we realize we are deeply known and loved by Him. We can count on that.

"Your love for one another will prove to the world that you are my disciples."

John 13:35 (NLT)

Chapter 02

joy

JOY | KA'OLI'OLI

As a child, I was amazed by this tropical flower that didn't grow in my Georgia yard. The hibiscus is not only the state flower of Hawaii, but a symbol of joy. Because the blooms typically last only one day, their vibrant, multi-colored and prolific flowers always remind me to seize the opportunity and be ready to find joy in the moment. The simple joy I find in this flower, its intricacies, and the attention to detail I see in how the Lord crafted it runs so deep that I even had one tattooed on my arm while in Hawaii last year. It's a permanent visual reminder that the fruit of the Spirit of joy is available to me each day—it's up to me to choose to find it in my everyday life.

> On my favorite beach, the ocean is a magical shade of blue. When you're standing knee-deep in it, the water is perfectly clear and you don't even realize it has color at all. As the waves rise, the transparent water turns crystal teal and then gives way to white foam as it crests, breaks, and crashes on the reef. Looking farther out, the light seems to dance all the way to the horizon on that ever-deepening water as it turns into a dark, azure sea. By simply looking at it from different

perspectives, the same water takes on vastly different colors. So it is with my life and outlook of joy. If I want to find joy, the Lord will allow me to see the beauty in my circumstances. If I choose joy and ask for the gift of His perspective, that can change how I perceive my situation. Not everything will be wonderful in life, but joy—true joy—can be found as long as we're looking.

joy

Those who live at the ends of the
earth stand in awe of your wonders.
From where the sun rises to where it
sets, you inspire shouts of joy.

Psalm 65:8 (NLT)

PART 01: FINDING THE FRUIT OF JOY IN THE WORD OF GOD
-Mary Magdalene At The Tomb-

YOU WILL SHOW ME THE WAY OF LIFE, GRANTING ME THE JOY OF YOUR PRESENCE AND THE PLEASURES OF LIVING WITH YOU FOREVER. —PSALM 16:11 (NLT)

She probably had to make herself go, to will her feet to move, to muster every bit of the strength she had to stand and walk to the tomb of the man to whom she had devoted her life. She had followed Him and believed He was the Messiah. The story that had played out right before her eyes over the last three years had led to this one horrible day. Now the story, seemingly, was over.

I imagine her face was still swollen from crying. It was the day after the Sabbath, but she probably had gotten little rest. She was exhausted—physically and mentally—and her Spirit was crushed. She was with two other women, but likely few words were spoken between them as they walked.

Only knowing glances.

Furrowed brows.

Tear-stained faces.

They were carrying spices and ointment used for burial preparation and the weight of broken hearts.

She found herself trying to be cordial to a man she thought to be the gardener who might have run off with Jesus' body. However, considering everything that had happened, it was all so confusing, and she couldn't think straight.

She could still hear Jesus' voice echoing in her ears, "You have sorrow now, but I will see you again and then you will rejoice; and no one can rob you of that joy" (John 16:22 TLB).

Joy? How could she have joy right now when Jesus was dead? Joy was nowhere to be found.

Until He called her name.

"Mary."

Imagine with me. She's a mess. Crying. Then, the man simply says one word that unlocks her. Her eyes widen, she gasps, turns quickly, and looks at Him—really looks at Him.

"Mary!" Jesus said. She turned toward him. "Master!" she exclaimed. John 20:16 (TLB)

She knows the cadence of her name on His lips.

It *is* Him!

Overwhelming joy.

Most translations note that Mary turned around when He said her name.

Sometimes, we can't see joy unless we intentionally look for it. Jesus was there all along; she just needed to refocus her attention and allow herself to experience the joy that was right before her eyes.

In verse 18, she declares, "I have seen the Lord, and this is what He said to me..." (VOICE)

When she saw Him—truly saw Him—it changed everything. Likewise, when we get a glimpse of true joy, it changes us, too.

The way we see joy can help us redefine our situations. It's a choice. Joy isn't a feeling. It's a condition of our hearts and the evidence of the Spirit of God working in our lives. It isn't an emotion that happens when something goes our way; that's happiness (which is lovely, but temporary). Joy is a decision we make in our hearts to mirror the heart of Jesus. Happiness is fleeting and fickle and is here today, gone tomorrow. Joy, however, can be the undercurrent in our lives, even when things seem to be falling apart.

Joy is the companion that remains even when happiness goes home.

James even tells us, "Consider it pure joy, my brothers and sisters, whenever you face trials of many kinds, because you know that the testing of your faith produces perseverance"

(James 1:2-3 NIV).

So how can we, like Mary, learn to focus on the joy right in front of us—even if the joy in the situation is really hard to find?

We simply need intentional time in His presence.

In the Psalms, it reads, "You will show me the way of life, granting me the joy of your presence and the pleasures of living with you forever" (Psalm 16:11 NLT).

Whatever moment we're in can be filled with joy if we pause to recognize His presence.

Mary's emotions were beyond "happy." I'm sure she was thrilled. However, the bedrock underneath that explosive moment of recognition was the joy of knowing that Jesus was *with* her. He was who He said He was, and as C.S. Lewis said, made "death work backward."[4]

This was not just a happy, emotive moment. This was *joy*.

The kind of joy that Jesus desires us to have is always tied to the fruit of love working itself out in our lives. As we saw in the last chapter, in John 15, Jesus tells the disciples why love is so important: "I have told you this so that you will have the same joy that I have. I also want your joy to be complete" (John 15:11 NIRV).

More love = more joy. The more we stay connected to the Father and abide in Him, the more joy we will have. Jesus offered us the perfect example of this by choosing to stay in constant connection with His Father. He declared that abiding in the love of God would allow us to experience the same joy that

He had. The same joy! Anytime I can do what Jesus did and receive what He promises, that's what I'm after!

Jesus encouraged His disciples (and us) to follow His example, to choose to obey the Father's commandments and receive His love. If we do that, Jesus says, this is where He finds His delight—His joy!

Since joy is a choice, I say let's choose radical joy. (You know, the kind that makes people stop and wonder a little tiny bit about you.) Psalm 33:3 encourages us, "Sing to Him a new song; play each the best way you can, and don't be afraid to be bold with your joyful feelings" (VOICE).

That's the kind of deep-seated joy that Mary likely felt. This is also the kind that Jesus embodied[5] as He stared down the enemy, looked death in the face, walked out of a grave, and even now, calls our name.

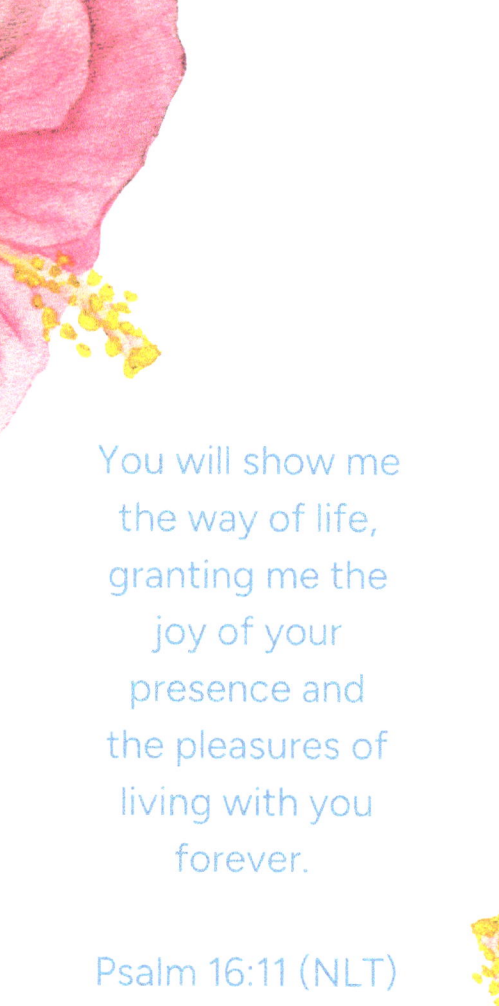

You will show me
the way of life,
granting me the
joy of your
presence and
the pleasures of
living with you
forever.

Psalm 16:11 (NLT)

TLB

PART 02: FINDING THE FRUIT OF JOY IN THE WORLD
-The Dryer-

SHOUT FOR JOY TO THE LORD, ALL THE EARTH. --PSALM 100.1 (NIV)

I love a good do-it-yourself project. I'm not afraid of a broken appliance or something around the house that needs to be fixed. It's not that I am some super handywoman; it's just that I have a hard time paying for a repair on something that, with a bit of elbow grease, a Google search, and YouTube, I can do myself. (As a side note, my mother says, "I do it myself," was one of the first phrases I ever said. God bless my precious, patient parents and husband.)

Plus, DIY projects have a beginning and an end, and I absolutely love to complete a project or a to-do list. (Can I get an "Amen" from all my fellow task-oriented people?) So, when the washer and dryer set we'd had for 18 years started acting funny, I sprang into action to see if I could fix it.

Over the years, I have replaced several parts on them and done what I could to make repairs. However, when water began pouring out of the bottom of the washer, I realized that despite what YouTube said, it was time to admit defeat and replace it.

Since it was a matching set and this one had seen a good run, we decided to scrap the washer and sell the working dryer. Then, off to Lowe's, we went.

After comparing models and gasping at prices that did not match those we found 18 years ago, we settled on a new stackable set and planned the delivery and installation.

A few days later, when I was doing my first load of laundry, something surprising happened.

At the end of the cycle, the dryer played a 15-second song. Hearing it, I literally laughed out loud. Fifteen seconds! That's a long time for an appliance to be making noise. My previous dryer simply buzzed when the load finished, and, honestly, it was abrasive. It was as if it was saying, "Look, I've done my part, now get in here."

This set, SINGS. It's the happiest little tune. As a musician, I cannot tell you how much I appreciate the satisfying little hook that starts on the 5, makes a little circular progression, and neatly lands on the 1. (IYKYK).

Let me tell you, it has brought me so much joy. It seems so trivial that the manufacturer made the dryer sing, *but I think that might be the point.*

I am well aware that the dryer has no soul or emotions. However, if we were comparing the old and the new dryers, the new one would certainly be choosing joy! Singing about something as mundane as the end of the drying cycle proves that something ordinary can be turned into something extraordinary.

I can only imagine the engineers in a meeting as they were building the dryer. "Hey, this could be fun. What if we made the end-of-cycle sound, a catchy little tune? It might bring people a little unexpected joy in their day."

That little song just reminds me to consciously acknowledge God's daily presence and provision and respond with joy. My other option is to go through life numb to it and not let any of the wonders change me. Joy is a choice.

No, not everything in our life is joyful. Not everything will be amazing or make us want to sing a fifteen-second song about some mundane part of it; however, it does beg the question, what normal thing *can* we reframe to elevate joy in our lives? What part of our lives have we decided, consciously or not, to exclude from experiencing the joy of the Lord?

Since joy is a choice rather than a fleeting emotion, let's harness its power in our lives in a way that reflects our gratitude for the simple things. And then, let's not keep that joy silent! Let it be the key that unlocks your voice to "shout for joy to the Lord, all the earth" and with all our hearts, "worship the Lord with gladness." Psalm 100:1-2a (NIV)

REJOICE IN THE LORD ALWAYS; AGAIN I WILL
SAY, REJOICE. —PHILIPPIANS 4:4 (ESV)

If you've spent a summer in the South, you know it's hot, y'all. The South does summer like an Olympic sport—each year trying to outdo the year before with record-breaking temperatures. It medals in "feels-like" ranges, scorching pavement, and UV indexes. I'm not new here. As a born-and-bred Southern Belle, I've done summers in Georgia and South Carolina my entire life. So even though I'm prepared, I'm also quick to find ways to cool off, be it a shaded front porch with a big glass of sweet tea (it really is the only way, darlin') or my new personal favorite, a Jeep ride.

A few years back, my husband and I had the opportunity to buy a vintage Jeep. It's a '73 CJ-5. We call her "Kelly." Although she has an after-market top, we rarely have it on since CJs are meant to be driven without them, and it's the perfect way to beat the heat.

She's a whole lot of fun, and I'm learning all about inline motors and wiring and little fix-it jobs, so I can do my best to keep her running. (I come from a long line of Southerners who did much more than tinker with cars, so I guess I get it honest. I wish my Papa Stanley could see me now.)

On one particularly gorgeous but sweltering afternoon, I jumped in the Jeep to cool off, disguised as a sudden need to "go run errands." Now, here's what you need to know about vintage

CJs. They are *loud*. The engine noise coupled with the wind noise naturally means if you want to enjoy your music, you have to turn up the volume. Plus, it's more fun if you want to car-karaoke (and I do, thank you very much).

As I was driving, the engine was humming, cars were passing me with their own music blasting, and the wind was roaring in my ears. Intermittently through all the noise and ever so faintly in the background, I could hear the song I was listening to, but I couldn't quite make out the words, and I didn't know which part of the song it was on. I wanted to sing along but couldn't hear it well enough to join in. All the other noise was drowning out the music I really wanted to hear. So, I turned it up.

It wasn't as if the song had stopped playing—the stereo was still on. And, it wasn't as if the sound couldn't be amplified more—the volume was simply not set at a level that would allow me to hear it above all the other noise around me.

That's when I started thinking about listening for the voice of the Lord. He is always speaking, but very often, my own life drowns Him out. I can't quite hear His voice as I should.

When life is loud, that's our cue to turn up our awareness of joy in our lives and be intentional about being tuned into His presence. And remember that in His presence there is fullness of joy! (Psalm 16:11).

Even over the noise, the Lord spoke to me quietly and asked me to "turn up" my awareness of His presence, to be more sensitive to the sound of His voice, and to fight for joy above the noise of life.

When I hear every other sound except the singular voice of my Father, who sings His love over me, it's my job to tune in to His voice and tune out the rest. When I have too much of the world blasting in my ears, it's my responsibility to turn it down. It's not a matter of "Is He speaking?" It's always a matter of "Are we listening?" When we quiet ourselves to hear Him, that's where we can find joy in His presence.

We all experience the noise of life trying to drown out our joy. When it does, let's take intentional measures to focus on the voice of the Lord and amplify joy in our lives so that our lives can sing along with His.

Tune our hearts, God, to your presence and the joy we find there. May we be found listening.

Shout for joy to the Lord, all the earth.

Psalm 100:1 (NIV)

Chapter 03

peace

PEACE | KE KU'IKAHI

The older we get, the more our hearts are marked by the experiences and trials we've been through—things that might have scarred us. However, those very things and our response to how we allow the Lord to use them can make our lives so beautiful. This makes me think of the Hawaiian monstera. It has a heart-shaped leaf that starts out green, glossy, and whole but doesn't stay that way. As they grow, the leaves tear and are filled with the characteristic holes that make them so lovely. The monstera doesn't resist those changes as it grows; it's actually what makes the leaves more beautiful! They peacefully surrender to the Creator's growth process. This heart-with-holes leaf reminds me of our own hearts that often carry the scars of past experiences. If we surrender to the Lord's work in our lives and allow His peace to fill us in the process, He can use those experiences to *transform* our lives.

I'm not a pink girl. I gravitate to neutrals, grays, and blacks; my wardrobe and home tend to reflect that. Although, there is something magical about the color the sky turns on a summer night when the sun starts to go down. My family knows to keep their eyes to the west around dinner time and alert me if I'm busy cooking and I'm missing the sky showing off through the front windows. I'm known to stop whatever I'm doing and shout, "Look at the sky!" I often take off my shoes, run to the front porch, and soak in the holy moment as the sky changes from a gentle pink to a vibrant heavenly glow.

My day may have been chaos, but those paused holy moments on the porch are a tiny kiss from the Lord, letting me know that He sees me, is with me, and is showing off His artistry to remind me of it all. When I see that pink, I sense God's peace and am reminded to slow down so I can grow in that fruit as well.

The Lord is my shepherd, I lack nothing. He makes me lie down in green patstures, he leads me beside quiet waters, he refreshes my soul.

Psalm 23:1-3a (NIV)

peace

"I am leaving you with a gift—peace
of mind and heart. And the peace I
give is a gift the world cannot give. So
don't be troubled or afraid."

John 14:27 (NLT)

PART 01: FINDING THE FRUIT OF PEACE IN THE WORD OF GOD
-Jesus Calming The Storm-

AND HE AWOKE AND REBUKED THE WIND AND SAID TO THE SEA, "PEACE! BE STILL!" AND THE WIND CEASED, AND THERE WAS A GREAT CALM. —MARK 4:39 (ESV)

The wind suddenly picked up. Peter brushed his long dark hair out of his eyes, looked to the horizon, and pointed off the boat's starboard side to alert the other disciples. There was no way to avoid it. The sky was growing so dark so fast, and they were not even halfway across the Sea of Galilee.

Too far to go. Not enough time to turn back. Stuck in the middle.

Peter knew they were in trouble.

The wooden vessel began to rock violently. Wind howling. More and more water was coming up and over the gunwales and into the boat, and no matter how hard these fishermen-turned-fishers-of-men tried to row against the torrent, they made little progress. While this was certainly not their first "all of a sudden" storm on this lake, this wasn't going to be just a wet, rough ride; this was a *will we make it back to shore alive* situation.

In my imagination, I see all 13 passengers.

Twelve struggling under the weight of oars, the wild wind, and shouting over the sound of imminent danger.

One sleeping in the back on a cushion.

Twelve passengers freaking out.

One blinking away peaceful sleep as He awakens to the wind blowing against His heaven-kissed face.

All thirteen passengers were experiencing the same storm, the majority whipped into a frenzy like the foamy waves that poured over the bow.

However, the One was totally at peace and unfazed by the chaos all around Him.

Words matter to me, and I believe every word in the Bible is inspired by the Holy Spirit and is there for a reason. That's why this small section of Mark's gospel and his chosen details are important and give us a picture of just how peaceful Jesus was at that moment.

> And a great windstorm arose, and the waves were breaking into the boat, so that the boat was already filling. But he was in the stern, asleep on the cushion. And they woke him and said to him, "Teacher, do you not care that we are perishing?"
> Mark 4:37-38 (ESV)

Jesus is in the back of the boat, the stern, sound asleep on a pillow. He's not up front, staring into the panic and chaos and facing the storm head-on. No. He's at the back.

He's not worried. He's not trying to get the disciples to start rowing in a faster cadence like some motivational coxswain; He's sleeping—the opposite of what the disciples thought He should be doing.

Mark also took the time to note that he was asleep on "the" cushion, implying that it was part of the ship's equipment. Scholars suggest this cushion or pillow was a large sandbag, possibly leather, used for ballast that was stored under a raised deck in the stern. More than likely, that's where Jesus was sleeping.

Ballast, or extra weight, is added to vessels to help keep them upright in storms and make traveling more stable.

It was ironic that they were carrying the Prince of Peace in their boat, who was all the stability their lives would ever need. Not only that, He slept on top of the one piece of equipment on the boat that would make their vessel more stable.

He was not being negligent or inattentive to the storm; on the contrary, even in his sleep, He purposefully added the weight of His presence to the one physical thing that would keep them afloat.

He was the ballast. He was their peace, even in the midst of the storm.

Nevertheless, they were so focused on the storm they didn't recognize that He was already working to keep them from drowning.

When they woke Jesus, and He spoke to the storm, He commanded peace. The winds and waves heard the voice that created them and, out of obedience, submitted to His Lordship.

Jesus speaks to us in that same way. The Voice that created us speaks peace to us and beckons our souls to respond.

In Proverbs 3:24 and Psalm 4:8, the Bible says a believer's sleep will be sweet and full of peace because he knows the Lord is with him. This is why Jesus rebukes the disciples when He is awakened. He asks them, "Have you still no faith?" Mark 4:40 (ESV).

Jesus shows that even in His sleep, He trusts God.

A number of years ago, I was in Israel and got caught in a boat on the Sea of Galilee in one of these "all of a sudden storms," and let me tell you, it was no joke. Southern storms can be impressive, but a storm that seems to appear out of nowhere while in the middle of a sea, that is, for all practical purposes, a small ocean, is truly a daunting feeling. It was nighttime, and the temperate air quickly turned to a cold, cutting wind. Like the disciples, we were too far from shore to return, yet had too far to go to stop and wait it out. The only option was through it. We were being pelted with driving rain and buffeted by a furious wind and, although on a powered boat, were being tossed by the large, out-of-nowhere waves. I immediately thought of this story. Since that time, I have had a completely different appreciation for what they must have experienced that evening.

Back on my Southern front porch, I know I can experience a storm while at the same time being protected from it. Perhaps that's why I truly enjoy a good rainstorm—from the safety of my dry rocking chair. I know this is a beautiful picture of how the Lord wants us to experience life. There *will* be storms, but we can experience the peace of God in them.

I'm learning that the fruit of peace is not the absence of the storm but the identification of God's presence right in the middle of it.

And He awoke and rebuked the wind and said to the sea, "Peace! Be still!" And the wind ceased, and there was a great calm.

Mark 4:39 (ESV)

PART 02: FINDING THE FRUIT OF PEACE IN THE WORLD
-The Fig Tree-

"I HAVE BEEN WATCHING YOU BEFORE PHILIP INVITED YOU HERE. EARLIER IN THE DAY, YOU WERE ENJOYING THE SHADE AND FRUIT OF THE FIG TREE. I SAW YOU THEN." —JOHN 1:48 (VOICE)

Quite honestly, I'm the least creative "Creative" you'll ever meet. That's not to say that I don't have creative gifts; I do, but they just don't look like what you would think of when most people think of a creative person.

My creative gifts, outside (hopefully) of writing, look more like killer spreadsheets, attention to detail, logistics planning, back-end operations, quiet observation, and organization. Yes, I sing and love music, thought-provoking art, and dance that moves me with emotion, but I do my best work quietly, on my own, in total silence.

As an introvert by nature (as in, the Founder of them all), I can absolutely get lost in my own thoughts. However, I do know that the Lord, who made me without mistake, knows this about me and lets me do my best creative work right between my ears. You should hear the ongoing dialog in my head 24/7, filled with problems I'm solving, plans I'm analyzing, and projects I'm creating. From those thoughts, I step back into the real world on my own terms, and put my carefully calculated thoughts in their rightful place. I'm a thinker. And one of my favorite places to think is with my Bible open in my office.

I have a small bedroom-turned-office in my house where I write. The high ceiling and big bright window make it feel spacious and dreamy. It is my creative space. I have curated and edited the decor and meticulously selected what is allowed in and gets to stay in—art, design elements, pictures, and lighting. To me, it all matters. As a creative, my physical working environment is essential, and it either breeds or kills my creativity.

Several years ago, I got a fiddle-leaf fig tree for my office when Pinterest said they were all the rage. It was small then but has grown to over 10 feet tall and has several long, leggy branches. One hangs over my desk, the other over a small "thinking chair" against the wall. This chair is where I meet the Lord. It's where I love to read my Bible, pray, read other books, and sort through all those swirling creative thoughts.

Recently, while I was sitting there, I was reminded of the story of Nathanael and when he first encountered Jesus.

Jesus had directly called a man named Philip to be one of His disciples, and as the story goes in John 1, Philip immediately seeks out his friend Nathanael to share the news. Nathanael reluctantly joins Philip to "come and see" Jesus for himself.

When Jesus sees Nathanael, he says, "I have been watching you before Philip invited you here. Earlier in the day, you were enjoying the shade and fruit of the fig tree. I saw you then" (John 1:48 VOICE).

"Sitting under a fig tree" was a phrase synonymous with being in a place of contemplation or thinking, specifically about the coming Messiah.

Nathanael was sitting in the shade of a fig tree, not too unlike me, sitting in my little chair under my own fig branches.

It occurred to me that even in my careful decorating and planning, I had inadvertently created a place to sit under a literal fig tree, a place where I connect to the Lord and often think, study, and pray. As I sat in my little thinking chair, I had to giggle a bit. This is where I, too, "enjoy the shade" (or spiritual covering in God's presence) "and the fruit" (or the benefit of being there) "of the fig tree," just like it says in John 1:48. This is where I find the fruit of peace.

To grow the Spirit's fruit in our lives, we must stop long enough to contemplate the things of God and let Him speak to us. If you do not have a regular space and place to meet with the Lord, I would love to encourage you to seek one out. His peace will find you there, and just like Nathanael, we can know Jesus is watching us in love and wants to see us enjoy the peace He provides.

-Perspective-

I'm not sure about you, but I don't love to rest. Now, let me be clear: I do hold a black belt in napping, so I can crush a Sunday afternoon nap. Despite that ability, I still struggle to *truly* rest. I enjoy being active and always have a running list of projects I'd love to accomplish. As I mentioned, my brain rarely stops thinking, planning, and dreaming—it almost always feels like it is "on" and rarely "off."

For many years, professionally, I took all of that can't-stop-won't-stop activity to the extreme and teetered on the verge of burnout. In recent years, however, I have learned the critical nature of rest and the benefits of engaging in a true Sabbath. I have seen time and time again, when I place a priority on rest and honor the Lord with my calendar, I'm far more productive (and nicer to be around). It's amazing what happens when you implement the biblical command of six days and a rest rather than trying to do it full-steam-ahead with no stops, in seven. I've learned the essential practice of *choosing* rest.

But what happens when you don't choose it and instead are *made* to rest?

Made to? Yes.

Earlier this year, I sustained a serious concussion. I was under a metal table on my front porch, fixing its wobbly leg (again, me with the DIY projects), and didn't climb out far enough before standing up. The top of my head met the edge of the metal table and took me to my knees. It was a hard hit but not the worst I've experienced. Two years prior, I received a severe concussion in an accident on a ladder, and two years before that, yet another. Three concussions in less than five years is not a life choice I would recommend. And, as you probably are aware from professional athletes you hear about on the news, concussion symptoms compound—so even a lesser incident can bring about the fury of every previous collision combined. This is what makes concussions so dangerous.

I don't remember most of those first weeks. Stubbornly, I tried to power through and live life as usual. (Remember, I don't love to rest.) I thought *I've done this before; I know how this goes; I can do this.* But I couldn't.

Everything felt impossible. I was trying to continue the worship team consulting work I do with my company, but I couldn't understand the conversations. I was also trying to keep up with emails and texts, but I couldn't bear to be on screens of any kind. I was clumsy and slow-moving and very easily exhausted. Most heartbreaking of all, I was days away from finishing this book. But everything about reading and the editing and revision process made me feel dizzy and sick. All I could do was wear sunglasses constantly, hold my hands over my ears to evade every noise possible, and look out the window blankly—a lot. Finally, after weeks of not improving and a sobering visit to the doctor, he confirmed what those who love me had been saying. You have to stop.

He called it PCS: Post-Concussion Syndrome, a form of Traumatic Brain Injury. There was no timeline or quick-fix therapy to rush my healing. Outside of a miraculous work of the Lord, my injury would simply heal when it healed. I rebelled against the decision to rest. I had too much to do and too much I wanted to keep doing, but I did not have a choice. I had to stop.

Did the Lord cause this accident? By no means. But will He use it in my life? As much as I allow Him to.

"He makes me lie down in green pastures, he leads me beside quiet waters, he refreshes my soul." Psalm 23:2-3a (NIV)

At the time of this book's publishing, I am still dealing with symptoms every day, and, spoiler alert, this chapter is not going to end with a tidy answer on how I've received God's peace and how everything has worked out beautifully. Candidly, it has been a fight to finish the book and complete what I believe I've been called to do in this season. For all practical purposes, my life is on pause. BUT—here is what I love about being "made" to lie down in these proverbial green pastures: God hasn't made me lie down on the edge of a cliff, or in the middle of a freeway, or in the presence of lions. He has made me lie down (according to Psalm 23) in a lush, beautiful place, where I'm safe and He's near. He is tending to me in the way that only The Great Shepherd can. I have to trust, through it all, He is refreshing my soul. That's what rest does.

Does that mean I feel refreshed at the moment? No. Does that mean I am happy about everything? Not at all. However, if the Lord is making me lie down, I know He is restoring something in me. I have His track record of faithfulness to count on, and that alone in this season brings me peace.

Peace is perspective. It's being able to step back to see the whole situation, rather than only the details of it. If you are too close to something, you truly cannot appreciate or enjoy its beauty—it blurs and clouds our vision. (Try looking at this page with the book on your nose.) But, when we, with the help of Jesus and others, step back and see our situation from the vantage point of a little bit of time or through the lens of the Lord's plan, we can receive greater peace and gain perspective.

When I get too focused on all the things I cannot do at the moment, like drive or endure lights and sound or go to the grocery store without getting wildly confused, I lose perspective and peace. However, if I can look at the greater picture and my place in His grander story, this is where I gain His peace. I must remind myself that His plans for me are good and will give me hope and a future (Jeremiah 29:11). At the same time, I also have to remember that I don't get a pass on suffering just because I know Jesus (Romans 8:18, John 16:33). Taking hold of these things gives me the perspective I need from the Prince of Peace himself.

Through it all, most mornings, I find myself walking outside to my front porch and sitting with my coffee at the table that took me down. (The table and I are still working on a peace agreement.)

I still have many unanswered questions. In time, answers will come—or—not. In the meanwhile, I'm searching for the Lord's viewpoint at this table set before me—the table of His perspective—this table of peace.

Chapter 04

patience

PATIENCE | KE AHONUI

Ginger is not what I would call a "cookie-cutter" plant. Its flowers are so diverse that one variety can look like a beehive, while another resembles a torch, or even a cone! Isn't God's creativity amazing? Remarkably, they are easy to grow and long-lasting. (Those reasons alone make them some of my favorites.)

To help us nurture the fruit of patience, God makes use of our different experiences, circumstances, and seasons of life. Like the wide variety of ginger flowers, our growth is never a one-size-fits-all. Patience might look one way with our spouse, another with a co-worker, another with our kids, and even with ourselves. Each type is beautiful and complex, and hopefully, each type we use helps to point back to the Creator as it grows in us.

> For gold to be refined, it has to undergo intense heat. It has to be melted down, where all the impurities are brought to the surface and burned off. This is a slow, careful process. The "gold" in my life is best seen when I'm patient enough to let God do the work He needs to do in me, to refine me, and burn off anything that

doesn't mirror His character. Growing in the fruit of the Spirit of patience is slow work. The color gold reminds me to be willing to wait for what is best as I submit myself to the heavenly purifying process, which, in time, makes me look more like Him.

But these things I plan won't happen right away. Slowly, steadily, surely, the time approaches when the vision will be fulfilled. If it seems slow, do not despair, for these things will surely come to pass. Just be patient! They will not be overdue a single day!

Habakkuk 2:3 (TLB)

patience

The Lord is compassionate and gracious, slow to anger, abounding in love. He will not always accuse, nor will he harbor his anger forever; he does not treat us as our sins deserve or repay us according to our iniquities. For as high as the heavens are above the earth, so great is his love for those who fear him; as far as the east is from the west, so far has he removed our transgressions from us.

Psalm 103:8-12 (NIV)

BUT LORD, YOU ARE A GOD FULL OF COMPASSION, GENEROUS IN GRACE, SLOW TO ANGER, AND BOUNDLESS IN LOYAL LOVE AND TRUTH. —PSALM 86:15 (VOICE)

The city was in an absolute uproar. It was noisy at the fire, where servants and guards alike were talking over one another and keeping themselves warm. Over the noise, Peter heard a sound, a common one he often ignored. But this time, it cut through the chaos like a knife and jolted him out of his conversation mid-sentence. It was the sound of a rooster crowing.

Marc Turnage, my friend and well-respected biblical scholar, suggests it wasn't an actual rooster, but The Rooster: someone who would blow a trumpet to signal the beginning of the work day at the temple.[6]

Regardless—human or chicken—the sound marked time.

Just hours before, Peter had sworn on his life that he would be faithful to Jesus. Now, he was living in the reality that he had not only denied knowing Jesus once, but *blatantly* three times—all before the rooster crowed. The hour had arrived and Peter had done exactly what Jesus said he would do.

To Peter, it must have felt like his heart was being ripped out of his chest. How could he have responded in fear after all Jesus had done for him? After all he'd seen?

It couldn't be said that he didn't hear the people's questions. It couldn't be said that he misunderstood what they were asking. He heard them, every one, three separate times, and all three times, he lied about his affiliation with the One who came to set all things right.

Peter was zealous and passionate. There was no denying that he was all-in. This bold fire within him made it easy for him to drop his fishing nets, apprentice with Jesus, and follow Him with a band of brothers for three years. This was Peter at his best.

But these same fiery characteristics, when fueled by fear, caused him to be impulsive, brassy, and unwilling to go down without a fight. Just the night before, he had cut off the ear of a man who had threatened Jesus.

Even still, Peter's passion was part of the reason Jesus loved him so much, why He called him, and wanted to build His church upon Peter's example.

Now standing by the fire, Peter was scared out of his mind and swearing to three different people that he was not a follower of Jesus, who was facing imminent trial. This was Peter at his worst.

As if the realization of his failing wasn't enough, as the words fell from Peter's lips, full of cursing as they came, he looked up and away from the eyes of those questioning him and straight into the eyes of Jesus. (Luke 22:61)

Patient love instantly confronted Peter's sin.

With nowhere to run and all his ugly, awful humanness on display, Peter instantly broke down. There was no hiding it.

Everyone had heard his outright denials, including The One man to whom he had promised his life.

All four gospel accounts record Peter's triple-declared denial. This explains why, hours earlier at the Last Supper, Jesus had looked at Peter directly and told him that He was praying for him specifically to be strong (Luke 22:32).

Jesus knew he would need it. Jesus knew what was coming.

After the rooster crowed, Peter wept uncontrollably at the reality of what he'd done. He had denied knowing Jesus. Three times asked. Three times denied. He was a traitor.

Several days after the crucifixion, we see the grace and patience of Jesus come full circle in Peter's life. The miraculously risen Savior is fixing breakfast for His friends on the beach, complete with fish on the fire and bread to share.

When they had finished eating, Jesus said to Simon Peter, "Simon son of John, do you love me more than these?" "Yes, Lord," he said, "you know that I love you." Jesus said, "Feed my lambs." Again Jesus said, "Simon son of John, do you love me?" He answered, "Yes, Lord, you know that I love you." Jesus said, "Take care of my sheep." The third time he said to him, "Simon son of John, do you love me?" Peter was hurt because Jesus asked him the third time, "Do you love me?" He said, "Lord, you know all things; you know that I love you." Jesus said, "Feed my sheep." John 21:15-17 (NIV)

Jesus asked him three times, "Do you love me?" Three times, Peter responded the same way, "You know that I love you."

You can almost hear the pain in Peter's voice. He knew he'd failed at a critical moment and with each question was reminded of that awful night.

Jesus wasn't forgetful or trying to be unkind in repeating His questioning. Instead, He was displaying the ultimate example of the fruit of patience with Peter.

He was allowing Peter *out of his own mouth* to respond in the way that he should have several days before. Peter is finally able to acknowledge, in front of others, that he knows and loves Jesus.

In this exchange, Jesus also reaffirms Peter's calling and empowerment as a leader. From that moment on, Peter's life is marked not only by a holy boldness but also by a humble wisdom that comes from knowing the Lord has been patient with him, his shortcomings, and his passionate heart.

What a beautiful display of patience. What a beautiful example to follow when the words or actions of others scar our lives.

In so many ways, I am like Peter—hot or cold. Either I am full-tilt in bold, zealous faith or find myself struggling to follow through in my day-to-day commitment to Him. In so many ways, Jesus is patient and reminds me that His grace is sufficient. (2 Corinthians 12:9), and the fruit of patience is the gift I need to extend to myself as I am growing.

Important to note: we shouldn't confuse God's patience in our shortcomings with His approval of the mess we've gotten ourselves into. In the same way He reassured Peter with His patient love, He reassures me that He will not leave me in my sins, failings, and lackluster devotion but will be patient with me because He is slow to anger and abounding in love.

> But you, O God, are both tender and kind, not easily angered, immense in love, and you never, never quit. So look me in the eye and show kindness, give your servant the strength to go on, save your dear, dear child! Make a show of how much you love me so the bullies who hate me will stand there slack-jawed, As you, God, gently and powerfully put me back on my feet. Psalm 86:15 (MSG)

So, as you and I grow in the fruit of patience, we have choices to make. Will we stay on this path long enough to see our lives transformed more into the likeness of Jesus, and will we stay near Him, close enough to learn the cadence of His character? Or will we short-change all of that and our spirit-filled development in the name of impatience, letting other things in our lives take precedence? I want to encourage you to "not get tired of doing what is right, for after a while we will reap a harvest of blessing if we don't get discouraged and give up" (Galatians 6:9 TLB).

When everything is going smoothly, it's easy to be patient with others and ourselves. But what do we do when faced with challenging and frightening situations and Jesus asks us to bear this fruit in real life? (Ugh. The worst.) Usually, we desire patience for ourselves and hope to receive it from others, yet we are reluctant to offer it. Or, we want to rush through our difficulties rather than wait for the time it takes to see patience grow.

We have to learn to be patient as He develops this fruit in us. Ironically, it takes patience to produce patience.

To produce something worthwhile takes time. Fruit does not grow on trees overnight. *It is produced.* (For crying out loud, I just read that it takes an avocado between 5 and 13 years to bear fruit. Good things come to those who wait.) However, if we are committed to the growth process, it is assuredly worth the wait. All of it makes us more like Him. All of it produces fruit in us.

I want the way I live to mirror the life, nature, and character of Jesus, and there is no shortcut to that kind of becoming. There is no 12-step program or 3-point sermon that will instantly make me more like Jesus. This is a lifetime journey of growth as I allow Jesus to be the center of my life. We won't be able to pick and choose what He wants to teach us. Yet, we do control the pace at which we learn it based on our receptivity to His leadership and our willingness to embody what we've learned as we strive to become more like Him.

The fruit of patience is hard to live out. While yes, it is very much about how we respond in encounters with people and situations, it also is learning how to show ourselves grace when we're not growing fruit as fast as we think we should be.

Fruit, as you know, starts with tiny seeds that are growing long before the evidence is seen.

And, if the God of Love, the ruler of the Universe, can teach me to be patient with others on the road to becoming more like Him, I can also learn to be patient with myself and my own growth. Even if, like Peter, I'm the one who needs it most.

But Lord, You are a God full of
compassion, generous in grace,
slow to anger, and boundless in
loyal love and truth.

Psalm 86:15 (VOICE)

BUT THESE THINGS I PLAN WON'T HAPPEN RIGHT AWAY. SLOWLY, STEADILY, SURELY, THE TIME APPROACHES WHEN THE VISION WILL BE FULFILLED. IF IT SEEMS SLOW, DO NOT DESPAIR, FOR THESE THINGS WILL SURELY COME TO PASS. JUST BE PATIENT! THEY WILL NOT BE OVERDUE A SINGLE DAY! —HABAKKUK 2:3 (TLB)

I'll be 50 years old soon. In the 37 years I've been journeying with the Lord, I have seen a distinctive pattern in my life when it comes to walking out the plans He has for me. I am always on some journey from "Point A" to "Point B" in my life. I see some "Point B" in my future, and I talk to the Lord about it and expect Him to get me from "Point A"—where I am now—to "Point B"—where I want to be—in a certain amount of time with a particular outcome. (I do a great job of trying to be the supreme ruler of the universe). Nonetheless, over and over (you think I'd learn), as He and I start on the path toward the destination I'm set on, I find that God often slows His gait as we walk. He's measured. Tempered. Patient. He doesn't seem to have His eyes set on the same "Point B" that I do, or the same timeline.

To me, His pace seems slow, off-timed, and maybe even uncaring, if I'm honest. Then, predictably, somewhere between weeks two and three of whatever journey I'm on, I get very impatient.

Lord, I've prayed. I've sought wise counsel. I've read your Word.

I know you have good things for me. Can you just hurry up and let me go have them?

I envision myself pulling the Lord along the road by the sleeve of His robe, feeling the self-created weight of my own impatience tugging against the beautiful, steadfast rate of His perfectly timed, sovereign pace. In my imagination, I see His eyes sparkle, and a broad smile appears as He, beautifully unbothered, lovingly laughs at my antics. This scene in my mind reminds me of a phrase from my book, *Waiting On Wonders,* that says, "fast is the enemy of deep, and deep work takes time." Boy, is that still so true. On those days when I want to rush the journey, the Lord reminds me that *time* is what I need to see this thing through, not a full sprint to claim what I think is mine.

He's never in a hurry. Never in a rush. Always on time. He is always perfect in His cadence.

Pausing patiently in His presence, even in the middle of the road to the destination, is where He wants us. Everything we learn there is what informs the growth of patience in us.

I am learning that His version of "Point B" is the *journey,* not the destination. He's more concerned with how I get from "Point A" to "Point B" in my heart than anything I could gain from simply arriving at a destination.

In fact, if I never arrived at this proverbial "Point B" but became more like Him along the way, He would consider our walk together a total success.

I think that's why the term "walking with the Lord" is so appropriate. It's not our *sprint* with the Lord; it's journeying with Him at a walking pace—slowly, intentionally, and in a way that helps us pause to notice the gold we would miss if we were running by. Jesus is the prize, not the pace on the path.

"Yahweh, you alone are my inheritance. You are my prize, my pleasure, and my portion. You hold my destiny and its timing in your hands." Psalm 16:5 (TPT)

Make no mistake: the journey with the Lord is not for the weak of heart. And if you want to journey easily through life, plain and simple, don't devote yourself to becoming more like Jesus! Traversing that path is tricky—and paved with the painfully unexpected, sheer cliffs, and certain detours. He will need to take you down some paths you probably wish you didn't have to travel. However, as we grow and discover the evidence of the fruit of the Spirit in our lives and learn to identify it in the Word of God and the world around us, it is undoubtedly worth every step.

Are you patient in the journey, or do you try to sprint ahead simply to get to the destination? Our Travel Companion, Jesus, can be trusted. He knows all the best places to see. He won't leave us when we get discouraged at the length of the journey or get frustrated when we try to press ahead without stopping to enjoy the needed slower moments.

Instead, He is lovingly patient with us and gently teaches us over and over that the journey is the destination—Godspeed.

-The Bowl of Chili-

ANYONE WHO IS PATIENT HAS GREAT UNDERSTANDING.
BUT ANYONE WHO GETS ANGRY QUICKLY SHOWS
HOW FOOLISH THEY ARE. —PROVERBS 14:29 (NIRV)

Road rage is real. I've had it and been the victim of it. (Not the violent or dangerous kind but the run-of-the-mill, frustrated-driver kind.) Let's be honest; most of us believe our way to drive is the right way, and everyone else has no idea how to do it. Funny how that works.

Here's proof: We would *nev-er* be distracted, look at our phones, or not be completely aware of our surroundings; that's only what *oth-er* people do. We would *nev-er* need grace as we navigate a new city, learn the nuances of a new car, or try to see the name of the road without our glasses on. *We* are the perfect drivers. Everyone else needs to move aside for *us*. Right? (Sigh.)

If we only had the same massive amount of patience for others as would fit in those monster Stanley cups we're all drinking from, we'd all be better off. (I digress, back to the plot.)

Several years ago, I planned to take a home-cooked dinner to a friend after she had a baby. I made a big pot of chili and put it in a disposable container so she didn't have to worry about returning dishes to me. It was very hot and very full, and the container was certainly not spill-proof. I knew it would be risky to take sloshing soup on a drive across town, but I like to live on the edge, so I put it on the floorboard of the car, and off I went.

As I drove, I realized I was gripping the steering wheel a bit more tightly. I was nervous. My turns were wide, slow, and intentional. One eye on the road, one eye on the chili on the floorboard. As I drove, people would pass me on the left and give me the obligatory "stare" as they flew by. As if to say, "I'm better than you. My driving is superior, and I'm showing you how intolerant I am of your slow driving by looking you right in the eyeballs when I pass by at top speed."

I had no choice. I had to drive slowly and carefully. Otherwise, the chili would have gone everywhere. I had hoped others would somehow miraculously understand.

That experience of delivering chili changed me in a way. Now every time I am in traffic and am behind someone going extremely slow or making very wide turns, I think, *what if they have a huge pot of chili on their floorboard?*

I could have used a ton of grace from other drivers that day when I was transporting chili. So, why am I not quick to offer that same grace to others? Do I know what they are going through? Do I know where they are headed or what precious cargo they are carrying? Or am I just so impatient to get to where I'm going that I have to stare them down to let them know they are, in some way, inconveniencing me?

We never know what people are carrying. What if they've just lost a parent and are overcome with grief? What if they have just had a baby and are driving home with their child for the first time? What if they are enjoying a really good song and are simply lost in the lyrics?

Why is it that we often have little patient grace for others, but we expect it from others in spades?

(Before you put the book down and get upset at me meddling in the depth of your patience, hear me; I am all of these things, too. I'm such a work in progress, and patience is the fruit of the Spirit that I probably need the most work in.)

How, then, can we learn to be more patient? Be aware. As we learn to identify and live out the fruit of the Spirit of patience, an easy, practical application of how to extend grace to others is to raise our awareness of our own desperate need for forgiveness and mercy, and then remember that others need that, too.

Psalm 53:2-3 is very clear about this. None are righteous, not one. Not even you and me.

When we're tempted to be impatient, remember that the Lord is patient with us and doesn't treat us as our sins deserve (Psalm 103). THANK THE LORD.

Let's find the fruit of patience even when we drive. Who knows, maybe the driver of that slow car is carrying hot chili to a friend in need, and their slow pace is actually there to purposefully remind us that the Lord is ever patient with us, too.

Anyone who is
patient has great
understanding. But
anyone who gets
angry quickly shows
how foolish they are.

Proverbs 14:29 (NIRV)

Chapter 05

kindness

KINDNESS | KA LOKOMAIKA'I

Okay. I'm going to teach you Hawaiian. Say it with me: pua (poo-ah), keni (keh-nee), keni (keh-nee). Puakenikeni. You did it! (If you want to learn more about the Hawaiian language and how to pronounce the fruit of the Spirit in Hawaiian, check out the "Learn Hawaiian" section in the back.)

In the early 1800s, island visitors could purchase this incredibly fragrant flower from lei makers for 10 cents. Thus, the small flower got its name from two Hawaiian words, "pua" - flower and "kenikeni" - ten cents. The small but mighty puakenikeni packs a potent punch and is considered one of the most fragrant flowers in the world. When someone in the room is wearing a puakenikeni lei, you know it!

This should be like us. When we follow Jesus, those around us should be able to identify the fruit-filled fragrance of Christ that we carry in our actions. Living out the fruit of the Spirit of kindness should set us apart. It should be undeniable that we have been with Jesus and are trying to pattern our lives after Him in the kind things we do and say. The fruit of the Spirit of kindness should be as evident in the life of a believer as the unmistakable fragrance of the puakenikeni.

From the time I was little, purple was my favorite color. (As mentioned, I'm not a pink girl, but purple? I've always been a fan.) When I was in middle school, my parents painted one of the walls in my bedroom a purplish-gray color, and I think I smiled every day for a year straight. I'm sure they didn't want a purple wall in their house, but out of kindness to me, they agreed.

Purple is also the color of royalty and reminds me of my King, Jesus. He could have rolled into Bethlehem with all the pomp and circumstance a king deserves. Instead, He humbled Himself and came as a baby, out of kindness to all humanity, to let us know that God understands us. There has certainly never been anyone more kind and worth emulating than Him.

Therefore, as God's
chosen people, holy
and dearly loved,
clothe yourselves
with compassion,
kindness, humility,
gentleness and
patience.

Colossians 3:12 (NIV)

kindness

Be kind and compassionate to one another, forgiving each other, just as in Christ God forgave you.

Ephesians 4:32 (NIV)

PART 01: FINDING THE FRUIT OF KINDNESS IN THE WORD OF GOD
-The Samaritan Woman-

"I AM HE," SAID JESUS. "YOU DON'T HAVE TO WAIT ANY LONGER OR LOOK ANY FURTHER." —JOHN 4:26 (MSG)

It was noonday in the Samaritan town of Sychar, not the time of day that a woman would typically gather water. The sun was beating down, and the well was some distance outside of town. She simply wanted to get her water and get back home without being bothered. She was used to the sideways glances and hushed accusatory whispers, but at this time of day, she could simply draw water, not attention. Yet even at noon, she still bore the weight not only of the stone jars she carried but of her choices.

As she approached Jacob's historic well, her eyes met those of a person sitting near it. She was surprised to find someone else there at midday. I imagine she was in no mood for a confrontation or a conversation. She quickly looked down to signal she would not engage in small talk and prepared to draw water quietly.

The person wasn't just a person. He was a man—a Jew. Likely, her least favorite combination.

Jews and Samaritans were arch-enemies. Their division and hatred spanned hundreds of years, with such racial and religious animosity between them that Jews were known to travel well out of their way just to avoid going through Samaria. Name-calling was regular: Dogs, Half-Breeds, Pagans. Neither group of people would ever purposefully choose to spend time with the other. And especially not in public.

This day would be different. This day would change everything for her.

She was shocked that the Jewish man sitting near the well initiated the conversation by asking for a drink of water. This act alone was far from acceptable. Social barriers were well established between men and women, and this conversation, in public, broke every imaginable social, racial, political, and gender norm of the day. She quickly established that she, a Samaritan, recognized Him as a Jew and that this was highly abnormal. He remained unfazed.

This was not simply a thirsty man at a well speaking to a woman ousted by her community.

> Jesus answered her, "If you knew the gift of God, and who it is that is saying to you, 'Give me a drink,' you would have asked him, and he would have given you living water." The woman said to him, "Sir, you have nothing to draw water with, and the well is deep. Where do you get that living water? Are you greater than our father Jacob? He gave us the well and drank from it himself, as did his sons and his livestock." Jesus said to her, "Everyone who drinks of this water will be thirsty again, but whoever drinks of the water that I will give him will never be thirsty again. The water that I will give him will become in him a spring of water welling up to eternal life." The woman said to him, "Sir, give me this

water, so that I will not be thirsty or have to come here to draw water." John 4:10-15 (ESV)

Jesus, in His loving kindness, connected something she wanted—water—with something she needed—a true Savior and the coming of the Messiah.

After starting one of the longest conversations recorded in scripture, Jesus asked her to bring her husband to the well.

> The woman answered him, "I have no husband." Jesus said to her, "You are right in saying, 'I have no husband'; for you have had five husbands, and the one you now have is not your husband. What you have said is true." The woman said to him, "Sir, I perceive that you are a prophet." John 4:17-19 (ESV)

He didn't do this to trap her in shame but to prove who He was in a way that was personal to her and would help her believe that all He had said was true. She was captivated.

An encounter with Jesus will do that to you.

He also addressed another hot topic between Jews and Samaritans—where to worship. Samaritans believed worship should happen on Mt. Gerizim, and Jews believed it should happen at the temple in Jerusalem. Jesus makes it clear that worship should not be focused on a place but on a *Person*.

> Jesus said to her, "Woman, believe me, the hour is coming when neither on this mountain nor in Jerusalem will you worship the Father. ...But the hour is coming, and is now here, when the true worshipers will worship the Father in Spirit and truth, for the Father is seeking such people to worship

him. God is Spirit, and those who worship him must worship in Spirit and truth." John 4:21, 23-24 (ESV)

Jesus not only engaged her in conversation but was also kind as He did so. There was no name-calling or hatred, just a desire to use this encounter to turn her world upside down.

"The woman said, 'I know that the Messiah will come. He is the one we call Christ. When he comes, he will explain everything to us.'" John 4:25 (CEV)

Jesus then dropped the proverbial bomb.

"'I am that one,' Jesus told her, 'and I am speaking to you now.'" John 4:26 (CEV)

It was no accident that Jesus showed up that day, at that hour, to that Samaritan woman. Nothing He ever did was without purpose.

This conversation was critical; it was the first time He had publicly announced Himself as the Messiah. Since He was the opposite of everything most people thought they were looking for, it was fitting that this exchange was so intentionally countercultural.

"I am that one."

He didn't announce it to people who were just like Him. He first came to those whom **most would consider** "the least of these."

That wasn't just a nice thing to do; it was kind.

There is a difference between nice and kind: Nice is cordial. Almost mechanical. Lifeless. Kind, however, is loving. Grace in action. A conscious act of compassion.

As I've studied the fruit of the Spirit, I see over and over the purpose behind the order of the list.

> But the Holy Spirit produces this kind of fruit in our lives: love, joy, peace, patience, kindness, goodness, faithfulness, gentleness, and self-control. There is no law against these things! Galatians 5:22-23 (NLT)

In a Spirit-filled life, everything starts with love and flows from it. And if that's the case, so should our actions. Kindness is no different.

Sometimes, though, our actions don't reflect loving-kindness at all. We think we're being kind, *but are we?* Maybe we don't want to ruffle feathers, so we say what is *almost* true, or we are afraid to give feedback to someone or encourage them in a way that might be hard to hear, so we sugarcoat the information and are unclear.

In these ways, we're simply being "nice" instead of kind. Being nice sometimes feels like the right move, but it doesn't allow the other person to fully experience the depth of love and potential growth that can come from genuine kindness.

Hear me clearly. Yes. Kind is saying what is true.

HOWEVER...

It must come from a place of love and encouragement and in a way that demonstrates other fruit of the Spirit in the delivery (like gentleness and self-control). Therefore, it's never harsh, accusatory, or cloaked under "I'm just speaking my mind." None of those things mirror the heart of Jesus. If our actions are rooted in selfishness, pride, self-preservation, or fear of confrontation, that's not kindness on display—quite the opposite.

Kindness always encourages, is good, and brings people closer to the Lord. *Always.*

That said, it was not Jesus being nice to include her in this momentous introduction as Messiah. It was *kind.* It was the Hebrew word "hesed," or loving-kindness of God, on full display. This conversation was a living example of the upside-down model of the Kingdom of God that He so often talked about. He was showing He had a loving relationship with all people—Jew and Gentile, slave and free, woman and man. No dividing lines, no hierarchy. She wasn't encountering someone being nice; she had likely gotten that response from the people in her community. Instead, she was experiencing true kindness, maybe for the first time in her life.

The conversation started at a well about water. It ended with an unsuspecting woman having an experience that ignited a fire in her that would spread through an entire town. It led her to tell them that everything they thought they knew about everything was getting **ready to change.** The Messiah had come. And did He ever.

Jesus never drew back from disturbing the stagnant waters of religion and shaking up the norm. He was stirring up change in the waters of the world as He brought the Kingdom of God to earth. Even as he disturbed the status quo, He was setting all things right.

Sometimes, stirring up the water and lovingly helping to change something for someone is the kindest thing we could ever do.

She no longer saw Him as a despised Jewish man asking for water. She saw kindness come alive right before her eyes.

After all, once you see the face of God, it changes *everything*.

Be kind and
compassionate to
one another,
forgiving each other,
just as in Christ God
forgave you.

Ephesians 4:32 (NIV)

PART 02: FINDING THE FRUIT OF KINDNESS IN THE WORLD
-The Umbrella-

IN RESPONSE TO ALL HE HAS DONE FOR US, LET US OUTDO EACH OTHER IN BEING HELPFUL AND KIND TO EACH OTHER AND IN DOING GOOD. —HEBREWS 10:24 (TLB)

It was pouring rain—the kind where not only the sky was gray, but even the air seemed gray as the sheets of water came down. Driving with my hazard lights on in a long line of slow-moving traffic, it was nearly impossible to see out the windshield as I crept down a main thoroughfare in my town.

It was so hard to see that I nearly ran over him before I ever saw him: a middle-aged man slowly walking on the side of the road. Soaked. He couldn't have been more wet if he had jumped into a pool. My heart immediately went out to him.

I wanted to pull over, to do something, but everyone on the road that day was having the same trouble seeing through the storm, and I was hemmed in by water of unknown depth on either shoulder. Stopping meant I was either going to disappear in a puddle or risk causing an accident.

I started to look for a place to turn around or stop and began to pray, *Lord, please help me find a way to help him.* I remembered I had an umbrella in my car, and while it wouldn't undo the deluge he had already been in, it would at least give him a bit of shelter to help him get where he was going.

I drove another half mile to a business where I could safely turn around and made the U-turn to go back to help him. It was now raining even harder, and although I looked and looked, I couldn't find him again. I felt so sad.

Lord, I'm trying to be kind. Not because I want to be some type of superhuman Christian, but simply because it's the right thing to do. Please help that gentleman and please give me another opportunity.

Have you ever wanted to be kind but weren't sure how to do it? What about when someone you know experiences loss, but you're unsure what to say. Or when someone is in a crisis of faith and you don't feel qualified to help them through it. Or when you are too quick to be hard on yourself and forget you're a work in progress, too.

Sometimes, kindness doesn't look like what you think it does.

Sometimes, it looks like simply sitting with someone who needs a companion and using no words. Kindness can look like texting a helpful Bible verse to a friend, knowing that the Word of God never returns void. You can experience kindness as you enjoy a sunrise, knowing that the God of the universe orchestrated that moment just for you and knew you'd be watching.

In its own beautiful way, kindness can also be what leads us to an awareness of our failings. The kindness and undeserved favor of God can lead us to understand the reality of our own unkindness and act as a meaningful wake-up call. It can shine a light on places we prefer to keep dark and help illuminate a new way of thinking. It can help us repent (Romans 2:4).

The kindness of God often looks like grace. I need it. You need it. We need to give it, watch for it, and be okay when others receive it. It is His to give and ours to try to emulate.

It's His delight to be kind and not treat us as our sins deserve (Micah 7:18). His kindness is there to lead us to make a U-turn, to turn from what we, in sin, choose and toward the right way to live.

Where in your life do you need to make a U-turn and choose a different kind of living simply because of the kindness of Christ? Where do you need to try to extend kindness to others, and where do you need to extend it to yourself?

Although I never did find the man I was looking for, unbelievably, ten minutes later, I saw someone else drenched and walking in the rain. God, in His kindness, gave me another opportunity to be kind to someone else. I lost an umbrella that day but gained a greater appreciation of keeping my eyes wide open to needed U-turns in life and how even those can lead us to a kinder type of living. Whether in love, in action toward others, or by the grace we receive from God, we can find the fruit of kindness in our lives and learn to give it away to others.

-The Airplane Row-

BUT GOD, WITH THE UNFATHOMABLE RICHNESS OF
HIS LOVE AND MERCY FOCUSED ON US, UNITED US
WITH THE ANOINTED ONE AND INFUSED OUR LIFELESS
SOULS WITH LIFE—EVEN THOUGH WE WERE BURIED
UNDER MOUNTAINS OF SIN—AND SAVED US BY HIS
GRACE. HE RAISED US UP WITH HIM AND SEATED
US IN THE HEAVENLY REALMS WITH OUR BELOVED
JESUS THE ANOINTED, THE LIBERATING KING. HE DID
THIS FOR A REASON: SO THAT FOR ALL ETERNITY
WE WILL STAND AS A LIVING TESTIMONY TO THE
INCREDIBLE RICHES OF HIS GRACE AND KINDNESS
THAT HE FREELY GIVES TO US BY UNITING US WITH
JESUS THE ANOINTED. —EPHESIANS 2:4-7 (VOICE)

Have you ever gotten something wonderful you didn't deserve?
Have you ever not gotten something you thought you did?

It had already been a long day. I was two flights in, worn out
from travel, and still had one more very long leg of a flight in
front of me before I would reach my final destination.

My first two flights had been completely full—not one empty
seat or overhead bin to be found. In fact, on both, the airline gate
agents were playing the bidding game, their urgency obvious
as their offers kept increasing in increments of $50 to entice
anyone who might want to jump on a later flight. You could see
people weighing their options. I had already decided I was not

going to be one of them. I would be making all my flights that day, no matter the amount of bribery or crowded conditions.

As I flopped down, exhausted, at the gate of my last flight, I noticed that even though it was set to board soon, the crowd at the gate for the upcoming six-hour flight looked thin. I've made this trip several times, and historically, this flight leaves twice a day and is *always* full.

Always.

I guess everyone is getting coffee or is in the bathroom, I thought to myself. And so I sat down, pulled out my computer, popped in my earbuds, and waited my turn to board.

Twenty-five minutes later, I was sitting in my tiny coach seat on the airplane. Even as a "fun-sized" human (as my 6'4" friend calls me), I still felt cramped and knew it would only get worse when the others in my row arrived. I had already mentally calculated the night before that if I wanted to justify upgrading my seat for more space, I would have to sell a large piece of furniture or a car on Facebook Marketplace to make it happen. So, with no upgrade possible, I was stuck where I was.

As I settled in, I began to mentally brace for how this flight would play out. I'd be at the window with two other stranger-companions squished like sardines for the next six hours. Ugh.

Resigned to that destiny, I pulled out my laptop again and tried to get the last bit of work done before taking off.

Five minutes later, the announcement came.

"Uh...Ladies and gentlemen, it appears that everyone is here, and the boarding door has been closed. Flight attendants, please prepare for take off."

If you've ever done any flying, you know what this means: you are in the clear.

When I heard the pilot's overly loud and slightly garbled announcement, I blinked quickly, shook my head, and looked up.

It couldn't be true.

Every passenger was on board, the boarding door shut, and I had the entire row of three seats to myself...for a six-hour flight!

I nearly burst into tears. Remember, I'm a fun-sized human—this means I can lay down nearly flat in a row of three airplane seats. I essentially had a first-class bed.

Giddy with excitement, all I could think to say to the Lord was, "I don't deserve your kindness!"

Kindness sometimes looks like getting something wonderful you do not deserve, like an empty airplane row. (And no, I don't get everything I think I want—not even close. Sometimes, life goes really sideways, or my motives are all out of whack, or it just doesn't work out for whatever reason.)

But kindness can also be *not* getting something you think you *do* deserve. Stick with me here...

There are things I know I deserve but don't get at all, like God's wrath. But because of what Jesus did for us on the cross, and because I believe in Him, instead, I get God's grace. He extends it to me time and time again, and the measure of grace He lavishes on me and the depth of His love in comparison with the depravity of my sin just doesn't add up.

I don't deserve His kindness.

I don't deserve it, and yet He gives it to me regardless. I don't have to work for it—I'll never be good enough, anyway—and it's nothing I can earn.

> For it's by God's grace that you have been saved. You receive it through faith. It was not our plan or our effort. It is God's gift, pure and simple. You didn't earn it, not one of us did, so don't go around bragging that you must have done something amazing. For we are the product of His hand, heaven's poetry etched on lives, created in the Anointed, Jesus, to accomplish the good works God arranged long ago. Ephesians 2:8-10 (VOICE)

There was no logical reason for me to have an entire airplane row to myself on a routinely busy flight. However, I didn't see it as a travel-day coincidence because I was aware of how the King and the Kingdom work. In some backward display of honor, He, instead, had rolled out the red carpet for me. I shook my head In disbelief as I experienced the fruit of His kindness in that moment. I knew, without a doubt, that it was from Him since it was consistent with the kind heart and unmerited love, favor, and grace of Jesus.

I am trying to be more aware of moments like this in my life where I have an opportunity to thank the Lord for His kindness and share that with others. Yes, I want to experience the fruit of His kindness in everyday moments, but I also want to live out an expression of kindness from a heart so full of gratitude that it has nowhere to go but to overflow to those around me. I want that to be true of me. I know you do, too. (That's so kind.)

In response to all he has done for us, let us outdo each other in being helpful and kind to each other and in doing good.

Hebrews 10:24 (TLB)

T_LB

Chapter 06

goodness

GOODNESS | KA MAIKA'I

I don't always have a green thumb, but orchids make it look like I do. Given the right conditions and a little bit of coaxing, they will rebloom and flower for months on end. Orchids are a fantastic choice for Hawaiian leis because even though they are incredibly detailed and diverse in colors and shapes, they are hearty and resilient and will hold the integrity of the bloom even after being picked. These long-lasting blooms remind me of the fruit of the Spirit of goodness.

Goodness is an internal quality we develop as our relationship and understanding of God grows. It is a reflection of who we are rather than something we add to our lives. Like the orchid, we can keep our integrity, "our shape," by not allowing ourselves to be conformed to the patterns of the world—but instead focus on God's goodness and character and let it strengthen us from the inside out. (Romans 12:2)

I'm not a fancy coffee drinker, and I don't like flavors or toppings or sweet coffee of any kind. But there is something wonderful about the simplicity of the right beans, roasted and brewed to perfection, with just a touch of cream. That is good. While tan itself isn't the most exciting color in the world, for those of us who love coffee, tan represents life-giving-elixir. With the right perspective, tan becomes much more exciting.

This is like goodness. Our life on its own isn't all that exciting without the addition of the fruit of the Spirit. We're just living a life that is kind of "tan." However, a life dedicated to the Lord and filled with the Spirit of God is one that is not only life-giving to us but also has the opportunity to bring life to others!

Surely your goodness and unfailing love will pursue me all the days of my life, and I will live in the house of the Lord forever.

Psalm 23:6 (NLT)

You are good and do only good; make me follow your lead.

Psalm 119:68 (TLB)

PART 01: FINDING THE FRUIT OF GOODNESS IN THE WORD OF GOD
-Moses On The Mountain-

SURELY YOUR GOODNESS AND UNFAILING LOVE WILL PURSUE ME ALL THE DAYS OF MY LIFE, AND I WILL LIVE IN THE HOUSE OF THE LORD FOREVER. —PSALM 23:6 (NLT)

It was a bold request, but Moses had a flair for the dramatic, especially when it came to displays of what God could do.

"Please. Let me see your Glory." Exodus 33:18 (MSG)

His *Glory*. Moses was asking for God's nature and character to become visible to him.

Risky. Even for a friend.

Somewhere along his journey with God, and within their declared friendship (Exodus 33:11), Moses felt confident enough to ask God to show him His glory.

It all began as Moses headed for the tent of meeting, which was way outside the camp, far from the living spaces, eating spaces, and places to gather. The tent of meeting was a special location where Moses met with God, alone. It was purposefully set apart.

As Moses walked by, people took notice. How could they not? They had seen what God could do and knew that if Moses was communing with God, something significant would happen.

Typically, as soon as he walked through the blue, purple, and scarlet embroidered fabric enrobing the portable sacred space, the cloud of Presence would descend, and then God would begin to speak.

But that day, Moses wanted to speak first. In my imagination, I can see him throw back the curtain dramatically, and begin to fuss at the Lord, lamenting even before making it to the center of the tent. I envision him throwing his hands out in exhausted aggravation and shouting at the top of his lungs in exasperation (and *maybe* even a little sass in his voice.)

> Look, You tell me, "Lead these people!" but You haven't yet told me whom You will send to accompany me. Yet You tell me, "I know you by name, and you have gained My trust and blessing." If I have gained Your trust and blessing, reveal Your way to me so that I can truly know You, and so that I may gain Your favor. Remember that this nation is Your covenant people. Exodus 33:12-13 (VOICE)

I'm so grateful we serve a God who can handle our honest emotions. Moses had a lot of them and often didn't hold back. Even still, God called him a friend. That gives me much assurance to know I am a friend of God, too.

God then promises Moses that His presence will go with them (Exodus 33:14), but that's seemingly not enough. *(Uh - seriously, Moses?)* Then, in the middle of what seems like a heated dialog, Moses drops the brassy request to not only have God's presence but to see God's glory in an *if-you're-really-going-to-be-with-me-then-prove-it* kind of way.

Whew. If I had seen that exchange in person, it would have left me speechless, with my mouth hanging wide open.

Moses is gutsy. He gives God this tongue-lashing and then, essentially says, *Oh yeah, since I'm leading these people and doing all this for you—now you're going to do something for me.*

Bold. This coming from the man who watched the Lord split the sea. Yes, Moses led the Israelites out of Egypt, but God had rescued them miraculously and dramatically, and *still* Moses is here demanding more.

We all have a bit of Moses in us. Just about the time the salt spray from the Red Sea dries on our faces from the last time God rescued us, Egypt-amnesia returns, and we get "too big for our britches," as my mama likes to say, and we start demanding things we have no business asking for.

Shockingly, God agrees to the request. (Remember, even in this, Moses is a friend.) God then replies that He will cause His goodness to pass in front of Moses. However, His goodness is so "good" that Moses will not be able to see it and survive, so God offers to hide him in an opening in the rock so that he can experience just a portion of it.

God's goodness is full of beautiful contradictions. It's kind and should not be messed with. It is righteous and sin-consuming. It's robed in love and risk.

> "You cannot see My face, for no one can see Me and live. Look, there is a place next to Me on the rock where you may stand. While My glory is passing by you, I will place you in a large crevice of the rock and hide you beneath My hand until

I have completely passed by. Then I will remove My hand, and you will see only My back. But you won't be able to see My face." Exodus 33:20-23 (VOICE)

God is equally blessing and protecting Moses. He's blessing him with the assurance of His presence in this miraculous display, but he's also protecting him from the intensity of His holiness.

Not only is God kind, He is good. These two fruits are sometimes referred to as the "twin fruits" because they reflect one another. Kindness is love lived out and seen in how you treat others.

Goodness, on the other hand, is a disposition of who you *are*. And when we're talking about God and His goodness, His glory, He is so good that if Moses were to have seen it, it would have taken him out.

Goodness is an inner disposition. It's not simply the opposite of "bad" behavior; instead, it is a quality of character or conduct that reflects purposeful choices in morality, purity, excellence, and righteousness.

It's who God IS.

Mirroring Moses' initial conversation starter, God responds, with His own version of, *"Look..."*, not in exasperation like Moses, but in a way that would allow him to be able to experience His goodness.

"Look, there is a place next to Me on the rock where you may stand." Exodus 33:21 (VOICE)

I love that line...*a place next to Me.*

The Lord, as He blesses and protects, never leaves us. This is a picture of His goodness in action. However, even in His "with-ness," He sometimes has to conceal Himself so we are not consumed. He wants us to experience the fullness of who He is, but He also knows our human limitations.

> In the same way, we can see and understand only a little about God now, as if we were peering at his reflection in a poor mirror; but someday we are going to see him in his completeness, face-to-face. Now all that I know is hazy and blurred, but then I will see everything clearly, just as clearly as God sees into my heart right now. 1 Corinthians 13:12 (TLB)

One day, *one day,* we will see Him face-to-face. We will know all there is to know, and He will not have to protect us from His own glory. But for now, out of His goodness, He chooses to shield us; shield us from seeing the big picture, shield us from knowing the entire plan, shield us from the details of every decision He makes, not because He's unkind, but because He's good.

So, I imagine Moses walking out of the tent, hiking to a nearby rock outcropping, slipping himself into a crevice, and waiting.

He's seen bushes burn. He's seen water rise in a wall. He's seen a staff turn into a snake, and bread fall from Heaven. But he has never experienced anything like this.

Exodus 34 describes Moses' entire encounter with God in detail. After seeing a glimpse of God, Moses stayed with Him for 40 days and 40 nights. He wrote down the Ten Commandments, and then returned to the people.

When he came back, Moses was different.

His face was glowing—so much so that his brother and the rest of the Israelites were afraid to get too close to him, knowing he had been with God.

Can that be said of you? When you've met with the Lord, is it obvious? Is your life somehow different when you do? And like Moses, do you have a space and place to meet with God? A place to lament, have big emotions, to stand in awe? A place where the path to His presence is well known and where you can experience His nearness?

There is no better place to learn about who God is than spending time in His presence. This is where the fruit of God's goodness is developed in our lives. This is how He changes us and makes us more like Him.

As we continue to explore the fruit of the Spirit of goodness and put it into action, ask yourself: Am I choosing purposefully to be more like Jesus in my decision-making and mirroring Him in morality, purity, excellence, and righteousness? *That* is learning to pattern our lives after who God IS. *That* is goodness.

FOR THE LORD IS GOOD. HIS UNFAILING LOVE
CONTINUES FOREVER, AND HIS FAITHFULNESS CONTINUES
TO EACH GENERATION. —PSALM 100:4-5 (NLT)

When my kids were little, we had "banned words" in the house. (Not necessarily the kind you're thinking, although we certainly didn't allow those either!) No, these were words that were way too often used, and because of this, they began to hold little meaning and lacked the weight that words should carry.

These words were "good" and "fine."

The exchange would go something like this:
"Ethan, how was your day at school today?"
"Good."
(Cue end of conversation).

Or when the youngest would walk through the back door:
"Hey, Brody, how are you?"
"Fine, how are you?"
(Cue end of conversation).

"Good" in this context told me nothing.
"Fine" didn't share any information.

They had become placeholders, not rich descriptive words. And, by now, you know I love words.

So, we started banning them. Of course, these "banned words" were declared so in the name of fun, and the boys were up for the challenge. And, because humor likes to ride in the sidecar of the fruit of joy, we love to have it come along on the journey whenever possible. The boys would come up with hilarious, extravagant responses that used every expanded definition of every word they could think of and all the sarcasm their brains could muster to describe their day:

> Oh, woman who gave me life, this afternoon at the location where I am educated was simply lovely. Those who educated me allowed me to offer answers to difficult problems, and because I utilized my mind in a positive way last evening to review the information, I am feeling quite positive about the numerical determination of how well I performed today.

Sigh. At least they didn't use "good" and "fine."

Maybe as adults, we shouldn't either. Or at least we should assign them carefully when we do. We all have words we overuse, don't we? That we're careless with?

Earlier this year, I decided that I was overusing the word "awesome." My coffee was awesome, your new outfit was awesome, and it was awesome to see you.

But the word awesome means "inspiring awe." The only thing that I know that does that is God. So, assigning that word also to my coffee began to feel wrong for me. It had become so overused in my vocabulary that it had lost all its meaning and power. I am now trying to reserve "awesome" for things related to the Lord or the work He has done. Those are the things that should truly inspire awe.

So, in its place, and because I'm a product of the '80s, I'm bringing back the word "rad." Feel free to join me.

I'm also beginning to get the same sense about the word "good." This little word is often overused and loses its full impact, especially in light of God's goodness.

We say school was good. But then we also say God is good. I'm pretty sure that's not the same thing.

Taste and see that the Lord is good... Psalm 34:8 (NIV)

Even Jesus restricted the word "good" to God alone:

> And as he was setting out on his journey, a man ran up and knelt before him and asked him, "Good Teacher, what must I do to inherit eternal life?" And Jesus said to him, "Why do you call me good? No one is good except God alone." Mark 10:17-18 (ESV)

Goodness is indicative of God's character and actions. Because He is good in every sense of the almighty-never wrong-always-right-and-righteous way, He alone can be good and call things good.

We see this in Genesis 1, where God declares each part good or very good after every perfected creation moment.

Keeping these things in mind, I'm also aware that His goodness has been chasing me down as long as I've been alive. Out of that goodness, He shows me mercy I don't deserve, love I could never earn, and an ever-presentness with me, no matter what.

When I reflect on that mind-bending truth, it's hard for me also to call my acai bowl "good."

Let's be mindful of the words we use! Let's be careful of attaching "good" to things that might be "interesting," "fun," or "incredible."

Will I still use the word "good?" For sure. Will I wrongly assign it to things not aligned with God's character and actions? Yes. But now that I have learned more about the fruit of the Spirit of goodness, will I think more about when to use that word and what I attach it to?

Absolutely.

As we grow in goodness and desire to become more like Him, let's be quick to declare that He alone is good. He alone is worthy of the weight of those words.

Oh, give thanks to the Lord, for he is good; his love and his kindness go on forever. 1 Chronicles 16:34 (TLB)

-Good Grief-

We've all lost something.

Keys. A shoe. A prized possession. A job.

But what happens when it's someone or something you love?

Grief.

Grief will accompany us all at some point in this life's journey. It will meet us in a moment, sneak up on us when we least expect it, but, in time, it can make us stronger if we're willing to hold hands with it, even when we don't want to walk the path it's taking us on.

Recently, we lost our family dog, and I have spent some time wrapping my heart around all the feelings. (And before you stop reading right here—this is not a chapter about losing a pet. It Is, but it isn't. And by no means am I here to say that this loss equates to the loss that some of you are dealing with or have experienced with humans you've loved. I've also had some of those losses, too.) Nonetheless, because I'm learning the art of slowing and learning to listen—loss of any kind is worth slowing down for and worth talking about. Because loss hurts.

Good Grief. Charlie Brown uses this phrase often in the PEANUTS comic. He uses it when he misses the football or whenever one of his friends does something ridiculous. But that's not the one I'm referencing.

This *good grief* means that no matter who or what we lost, we are experiencing grief because it means we loved. It means there was joy. It means memories were created that are worth savoring. It means we were privileged enough to share space with a living thing that the Lord created and brought into our lives for a reason. It is worth grieving over. And we should.

It is good, or right, to grieve.

So often, we want to power through hardship and loss and get to the other side of whatever is "normal," so that we don't have to feel vulnerable, express emotion, or continue to hold hands with grief. The process of grieving once again connects us with our finite humanness and reacquaints us with the jolting recognition that this is not Heaven—yet.

Right now, we live in a broken world where bodies break down and mortality of all things hovers at 100%. While I'm not here to debate whether animals are in Heaven or not, I am here to say that regardless of your stance on that, *all life*—human, animal, plant, or otherwise—is precious to the Father (Matthew 10:29-31). If He took time to create it, we should take time to honor it with our grief.

Make no mistake about it—the Lord is close to the broken-hearted (Psalm 34:18). Thankfully, He also doesn't leave us in our sadness or in the tension between what was, what is, and what will be, but instead walks right into it with us and counts all of that emotion just as holy as a moment of hushed reverence in His presence.

May you also be comforted to know that attending to grief and working through it, while hard, will produce fruit in your life that can bloom into something so beautifully good. As you do, the Lord will give you "beauty for ashes, the oil of joy for mourning, the garment of praise for the spirit of heaviness" (Isaiah 61:3 KJV).

Whether you are walking through unimaginable grief or aware that you will journey with it at some point, let this be a reminder as you process all of its essential stages that each one is important and has a purpose.

As much as you may want to move through the stages of grief quickly, let each one have its place, and give it time as you honor the one you've lost with the good grief that the Lord is allowing you to experience—thanking Him for the ability to love.

Every moment has the opportunity of being a holy one, even one filled with grief. If you're on the path of grief, He's holding your hand. May you be comforted knowing He is with you and has never been closer than He is right now.

"Blessed are those who mourn, for they will be comforted."
Matthew 5:4 (NIV)

Chapter 07

faithfulness

FAITHFULNESS | KA MANA'O'I'O

Okay, this is another tricky one. Say it with me: 'ohi'a (oh-hee-ah) lehua (leh-hoo-ah). 'Ohi'a lehua. You got it! The 'ohi'a lehua can be anywhere from shrub size to over 80 feet tall. Its creation is steeped in legends surrounding the Hawaiian goddess of fire, Pele.

Why? This tree is one of the first to push its way through dry lava fields after an eruption. It's fascinating. Because it fights to grow deep roots and has a miraculous ability to avoid toxic volcanic gas absorption, it can thrive in these severe and barren locations. And that's what I love most. It has a dogged determination to grow in a harsh environment and does not let the conditions around it hinder its growth.

We, too, can choose that kind of living. We can choose to grow the deep roots of perseverance and faithful dedication to the Lord. By staying rooted, loyal, and steadfast in our commitment to the Lord, we can bring beauty to barren places in the world.

Jesus taught us how the fruit of faithfulness can become evident in our lives. He followed the will of His Father, despite how our hostile world refused to accept Him. Nevertheless, His presence and sacrifice changed the world forever.

Many years ago, my dear friend, Liz, got me hooked on the color gray. She stained the floors in her house gray long before anyone was doing it, and I was smitten. It sounds crazy, but it opened my eyes to a whole new world of creative "other" colors and applications. You see, I tend to be logical, methodical, and calculated (and boring). I like things to be predictable...and, I'll say it, *safe*. Walls are white, wood floors are brown, brick is red. Liz taught me that walls can be teal, art can be full of whimsy, floors can be stained an unexpected gray, and bricks can be limewashed.

I've also found that God has created grays that are far more vibrant than just a lighter version of black. There is *gray*, like the color of the sky, right before it rains. *Gray*, like the color the ocean turns when the water goes all sparkly just before sunset. *Gray*, like the color of steel and platinum—of strength. Gray is anything but boring. However, sometimes life can seem "gray" in an ambiguous kind of way. It can be unexpected and unpredictable. For planners like me, these "gray" times can be just what I need to draw me back to the steadfast faithfulness of the Lord and to remind me that though life is rarely black and white, the Lord can always show up in the gray.

Jesus Christ is the same yesterday,
today, and forever.

Hebrews 13:8 (NLT)

faithfulness

The steadfast love of the Lord never ceases; his mercies never come to an end; they are new every morning; great is your faithfulness.

Lamentations 3:22-23 (ESV)

JESUS CHRIST IS THE SAME YESTERDAY, TODAY, AND FOREVER. —HEBREWS 13:8 (NLT)

Daniel entered the house and began to climb the stairs to his bedroom. He had a choice to make, and he knew it would place his life on the line. As he ascended, his resolve strengthened like steel in his spine. He would remain faithful to the Lord, "come what may."

Once in his room, Daniel shut the door and knelt on the rug near the window. He was not only placing his knees on the ground but also putting his foot down.

The window and his heart faced Jerusalem. He prayed here three times each day, and nothing would deter him from his singular devotion to God.

Not even a death threat from the King.

> Even though Daniel was aware the king had signed the ordinance into law, he continued to do what he always did. He would go home, ascend the stairs to the upper room—which had windows facing toward Jerusalem—and get down on his knees three times a day and pray to his God and praise Him. Daniel 6:10 (VOICE)

King Darius had just signed into law an edict that stated anyone who prayed to anyone other than the King, himself, would be put to death. And not just a run-of-the-mill death: it would be death by lions.

I can think of a lot of ways to go, but death by lions would have to be one of the worst.

This was not the first time Daniel's faith was tested. His devotion and consistency were evident in his teen years, when he refused to eat the food of his captors in Babylon and chose instead to stay faithful to the laws of the Torah.

> But Daniel made up his mind that he would not defile himself with the king's choice food or with the wine which he drank; so he sought permission from the commander of the officials that he might not defile himself. Daniel 1:8 (NASB)

Daniel made up his mind.

This was not a spur-of-the-moment decision; it was something he'd deliberately thought through and taken purposeful steps to follow.

This was faithfulness.

You don't just wake up one day and say, *"I'm going to be faithful today."* No. Faithfulness has a long track record. It has a history. It is a willing consistency to show up and do the thing—day after day, week after week.

When you choose faithfulness, one day, you will wake up and look back over the arc of your life, and you will not only see where you've been dedicated to your decisions, but also where God has been faithful to you.

Faithfulness cannot be hurried. It is a time-tested fruit that comes from doing what you know to be right, day after day, even when you don't want to or know what it will cost you.

I can't imagine Daniel wanted to be torn apart by lions. But I also know that he couldn't imagine not worshiping the God who had been faithful to him.

Not only was he known for his faithfulness, but he had grown up with a band of friends who felt the same way. (This is an excellent reminder that it matters who you run with.)

And even as his friends, Shadrach, Meshach, and Abednego, faced death by incineration, they boldly proclaimed,

> "Your threat means nothing to us. If you throw us in the fire, the God we serve can rescue us from your roaring furnace and anything else you might cook up, O king. But even if he doesn't, it wouldn't make a bit of difference, O king. We still wouldn't serve your gods or worship the gold statue you set up." Daniel 3:16-18 (MSG).

But even if he doesn't...

But He *did*.

And not only did God rescue them completely unharmed, but He elevated them to positions of power within the kingdom.

This is what our God does. This was their reward for faithfulness. And Daniel remembered it.

With the echoes of his friends' brassy statements still ringing in the air from years before, and the sound of lions roaring in the distance, Daniel faced Jerusalem, looked out his window, knelt to the ground, and responded in the only way he knew how: worship.

When faced with a normal day, he worshiped.

When faced with what could have been his last day, he worshiped.

When Daniel faced this incredibly difficult crossroads moment, his faith remained unwavering. Daniel stayed faithful to the one true God. With his heart fully committed, Daniel's muscle memory of faithfulness kicked in. He prayed and worshiped and then faced lions.

I wonder if he stood before them boldly, or if he, at first, cowered and cried. Either would have been appropriate as he seemingly faced his last moments. But one thing is certain: when the angel of the Lord appeared and caused those lions to forget that Daniel was food, Daniel would once again have fallen down in worship.

Daniel was faithful to God, and God was faithful to Daniel.

We see this fruit in the life of Jesus over and over and over.

Steadfast.

"For I have come down from heaven, not to do my own will but the will of him who sent me." John 6:38 (ESV)

Committed.

"...but he said to them, 'I must preach the good news of the kingdom of God to the other towns as well; for I was sent for this purpose.'" Luke 4:43 (ESV)

And, knowing it would be hard—but the most necessary decision ever made—Jesus set His face like flint and endured the cross for the redemption of the world.

"Now it came to pass, when the time had come for Him to be received up, that He steadfastly set His face to go to Jerusalem." Luke 9:51 (NKJV)

From the time he was a child found in the temple (Luke 2:49) and every day thereafter, Jesus displayed the fruit of faithfulness toward His Father and the ministry that was before Him.

Never once did He hesitate. Never once did He consider giving up on the plan for "Operation: Rescue Humanity." And while it was not an easy decision, but one He sweated blood over, He chose to be faithful over His own preferences and comfort. He lived His life in alignment with His Father, displaying a steady love and devotion that ultimately would liberate everyone in the world who chose to believe in Him.

...His example is this: Because His heart was focused on the joy of knowing that you would be His, he endured the

agony of the cross and conquered its humiliation, and now sits exalted at the right hand of the throne of God!
Hebrews 12:2b (TPT)

When others bow to the world's standards...when life turns up the heat...when lions roar, be found faithful to the Father, and know without a doubt that God is always faithful in His commitment to you.

PART 02: FINDING THE FRUIT OF FAITHFULNESS IN THE WORLD
-Equilibrium-

LET YOUR EYES LOOK STRAIGHT AHEAD; FIX YOUR GAZE
DIRECTLY BEFORE YOU. GIVE CAREFUL THOUGHT TO
THE PATHS FOR YOUR FEET AND BE STEADFAST IN ALL
YOUR WAYS. DO NOT TURN TO THE RIGHT OR THE LEFT;
KEEP YOUR FOOT FROM EVIL. —PROVERBS 4:25-27 (NIV)

Before my latest concussion, I had started taking exercise classes again. As I mentioned, I'm almost 50, and while this number
doesn't really matter to me, my body is quick to remind me
that it should. You see, I took some time off from exercising. To
be clear, when I say I took some time off, I took 22 years off. I
used to exercise regularly before I had children and then #life.
My exercise became chasing babies and trying to walk the dog,
but that was it. (I do not recommend this as a life decision.)

All said, I enjoyed the process of getting back at it. I enjoyed
getting up early, going to class, and starting my day moving my
body. Part of what we did in the class was to work on our core
strength and balance. My parents enrolled me in various dance
and gymnastics classes as a child, so, thankfully, I had muscle
memory working in my favor and my balance was still relatively
good. However, when you're standing on one leg with your arms
in the air and it's pre-coffee hour, that's a whole other issue.
My instructors were kind and only laughed at me occasionally.

Something I remember from dance and gymnastic training is

what is called "spotting." If you are turning, spinning, or trying to set your balance, you are trained to find an immovable object and keep your focus on it as long as possible. As you turn, you fix your gaze on that object until the very last second, and then you turn your head quickly and "spot" that same immovable object again. (Imagine every ballerina you've ever seen doing fouetté turns). If you aren't spotting, you will lose where your body is in space and either get dizzy when you spin or fall over when you try to balance.

This reminds me so much of what we're called to do as believers: to keep our eyes "fixed."

"You keep him in perfect peace whose mind is stayed on you, because he trusts in you. Trust in the Lord forever, for the Lord God is an everlasting rock." Isaiah 26:3-4 (ESV)

"Trust in the Lord with all your heart, and do not lean on your own understanding." Proverbs 3:5 (ESV)

"Let us keep our eyes fixed on Jesus, on whom our faith depends from beginning to end." Hebrews 12:2a (GNT)

The Lord is our immovable object. Faithful. True. He can be trusted.

If we're busy spinning through our lives and don't keep our eyes locked on Him, our lives will spin us into a dizzy frenzy. If we are constantly distracted by our phones or what's happening over here or not happening over there, we risk losing our spiritual equilibrium.

One of my favorite Bible stories is found in 2 Chronicles 20.

It tells the story of King Jehoshaphat and his victory over his neighboring enemies.

Initially, he looked at the armies and their huge size and became afraid. He took his eyes off the Eternal. He lost his equilibrium. Even though he was afraid, he gathered everyone in Judah to fast, pray, and worship. Then, he cried out to God in honesty.

> Our God, will you not judge them? For we have no power to face this vast army that is attacking us. We do not know what to do, but our eyes are on you. 2 Chronicles 20:12 (NIV)

Eyes on God—steady.

Looking left or right—bound to go down.

I love his candid prayer: *"We do not know what to do, but our eyes are on you."* He was calling on God for help and reminding his soul to keep his equilibrium centered on God. It was the only way they were going to win.

Then, one of the worship leaders, Jahaziel, received a prophetic word from the Lord and told all of Judah, the citizens of Jerusalem, and the King himself to listen to what the Lord had to say to them:

> "Do not fear or worry about this army. The battle is not yours to fight; it is the True God's. Tomorrow, they will travel through the ascent of Ziz. Meet them at the end of the valley before the wilderness of Jeruel. There, I will be watching. Stand and watch, but do not fight the battle. There, you will watch the Eternal save you, Judah and Jerusalem."
> 2 Chronicles 20:15-17 (VOICE)

And with that, the victory was sealed.

> As they sang and *praised*, (emphasis mine) the Eternal was ready to cause great confusion in battle for the men from Ammon, Moab, and Mount Seir (in Edom) who had come to attack Judah. They were utterly defeated, turning on one another. 2 Chronicles 20:22 (VOICE)

That day, the weapon was worship. The battle was won within a song and through the power of God—as long as their focus was on God through worship. I regularly wield this weapon of worship and encourage you to take it up in whatever you face today.

When life seems—a lot—when you are unsure or don't know what to do, let this be a lesson for us all: worship your way back into equilibrium. Worship your way to victory. God alone is our immovable object. With our eyes set and focused on Him, we will never find ourselves out of balance.

-The Tides-

HE IS THE MAKER OF HEAVEN AND EARTH, THE
SEA, AND EVERYTHING IN THEM—HE REMAINS
FAITHFUL FOREVER. —PSALM 146:6 (NIV)

I have the joy of writing this particular chapter in Hawaii while staring at the ocean. The calming sound of the never-ending waves is my soundtrack.

I'm relatively sure I am the only person on the beach today who is writing on a laptop under an umbrella. But not only am I writing, I am watching.

I've come to know the pattern of the ocean at this particular beach very well. In the winter months, it has huge waves, and surfers come in droves to line up and have their turn to catch that ever-elusive perfect tubing wave. The roar of the waves pounding the shore is almost deafening. Offshore, they can be big enough for tow-in and 3x overhead. When the waves are that huge, just before they crest, you can see straight through the clear blue-green wall of water and then watch it turn into tumultuous foamy white power. It is otherworldly. Wave after wave comes in. Beachgoers marvel and point at the horizon and exclaim, *"Whoa! Look at that one!"* It's awe-inspiring.

Contrast that with summer months when it is as flat as a lake, and the only sound that comes from the water is the quiet lapping of the inch-high waves creeping on shore. It's so quiet, I can hear sea birds chirping and children laughing. It's peaceful. The water is clear, quiet, and still.

Winter or summer, bringing a tumultuous or calm surf, the tides are consistent. They do change every 6 hours—from low to high and high to low—but even that is predictable, and you can literally set your watch by it.

The tide rolls in and out. Every day. Without fail. Faithful.

The tides can teach us a lot about faithfulness. God created the tides, and since everything He created is meant to point back to Him (Romans 1:20), naturally, even the tides and their predictable patterns point back to His faithful characteristics.

Even as steady as the tides are, the Lord is even more faithful. We can count on Him to see us through, to never leave us, to walk with us, protect us, and guide us.

Not only will He be faithful to us, but His faithfulness will live on in the lives of our children, and their children, and theirs if our hearts are set on His.

"For the Lord is always good. He is always loving and kind, and his faithfulness goes on and on to each succeeding generation." Psalm 100:5 (TLB)

Isn't that comforting to know? As sure as the tides, He is always good. Always loving and kind. And faithful forever.

Not just when He feels like it. Not just when it suits Him. But always.

"Always" is a big word. It means—well, always. There are things I do sometimes or occasionally, but there are very few that I do "always." That list actually might just be limited to breathing and having a heartbeat. Until I don't.

God, however, is an "always" kind of God. He always displays every fruit perfectly. He has impeccable timing, even when we might think it's off. (Go back and read the chapter on Patience). He is evergreen and can be trusted. Knowing that we get to serve a God who is always all of these things makes me want to do all I can to mirror His example.

Will I always be loving or kind as a wife? No. Will I always show gentleness and carry an attitude of peace in my parenting? No. Will I be an always-faithful friend? No. Just remember, the goal is to actively grow and pattern our lives after the fruit we see displayed so perfectly in His. It's okay to be a work in progress.

Like the tides, may our lives mirror the faithful predictability of our Father.

Chapter 08

gentleness

GENTLENESS | KE AKAHAI

Ever heard of poi? It's a grayish-purple paste made from steamed and pounded taro root. You either love it or hate it. (I had a chance to make poi on my last trip to the islands, and my fingertips were stained purple for days.) Here are a few facts I learned from the locals while we made poi: Taro is known as "the potato of the tropics." The large leaf, also known as elephant ears, can grow to be six feet tall. It's grown in fields covered in water and has so many nutritional benefits. The roots can be cooked and made into chips, and the leaves can be wrapped around pork for a traditional Hawaiian meal (lau lau pork - YUM). Interestingly, raw taro roots and leaves are poisonous, but the toxins are completely neutralized when cooked. This reminds me of how our words, lives, and actions, which can be used for so many beneficial things, can be toxic to others if not properly covered in the Spirit-filled characteristics of gentleness. It doesn't matter who we are or what we can do if our lives hurt others. Jesus was a gentle, all-powerful, yet calm presence who treated others as they should be treated. This is gentleness.

The water in Hanalei Bay on Kauai turns a bluey-green color in mid-April that I've tried so many times to capture in photos, words, and paint chips. I've tried to describe it to people, but it's mysteriously evasive. Too blue, and it goes marine; too green, and it goes mint. I even had a hard time getting it right in the book. Teal is known to be calming, and I'd be the first to agree as I look at that color in the water on a cloudless day from the vantage point of my beach chair. There is something about the clear teal color of the sea that just seems gentle. (The ocean, mind you, is not. It will absolutely take you out.) But when the water is that color, and you can stand in it waist-deep and see right through it to your toes, there seems to be a soft, gentle quality to it. This reminds me of Jesus' strong and calm presence that feels safe and yet must be respected. To me, teal is gentle.

"Accept my teachings and learn from me, because I am gentle and humble in spirit, and you will find rest for your lives."

Matthew 11:29 (NCV)

gentleness

Let your gentleness be evident to all.
The Lord is near.

Philippians 4:5 (NIV)

PART 01: FINDING THE FRUIT OF GENTLENESS IN THE WORD OF GOD
-Casting The First Stone-

"ACCEPT MY TEACHINGS AND LEARN FROM ME, BECAUSE
I AM GENTLE AND HUMBLE IN SPIRIT, AND YOU WILL
FIND REST FOR YOUR LIVES." —MATTHEW 11:29 (NCV)

Their hands are tight on her arm, pulling her through a crowd at the Temple. The Pharisees and scribes have the adultress in one hand and large stones in the other.

They shout accusations at her, causing a commotion as they go. The more they shout, the more people come, carrying their own stones, ready to join in.

The dust kicked up along the road builds as the men roughly lead her to where Jesus is seated, teaching a crowd.

The woman, thrust right in front of Jesus, stumbles as she is pushed forward. Just as she regains her balance and stands up straight, she finds herself eye-to-eye with the Teacher. He pauses. The dust settles. The accusers then begin to shout.

"'Teacher,' they said to Jesus, 'this woman was caught in the act of adultery. The law of Moses says to stone her. What do you say?'" John 8:4 (NLT)

The Pharisees and scribes have no time for, "Excuse me, Jesus. We hate to bother you, but what do you think about this scenario?"

No. They have come for blood.

She's guilty, and this is undoubtedly going to be death for her and, depending on His response, possibly also for Jesus. It was a trap set to kill them both.

If Jesus doesn't condemn her sin, He's not upholding the law of Moses and will be seen to speak against God's justice. If He does condemn her, He is going directly against all of His own teachings about love and what the Kingdom of God looks like.

The woman says nothing.

She knows she's guilty, and she knows what that means. The law is clear, and she has seen it enacted before. There would be no getting out of this. All she can do is stand there with tears streaming down her cheeks, her sin at the epicenter of this object lesson.

Jesus stoops down and begins to draw in the dirt. The Pharisees and scribes continue to press Jesus.

What are you going to do about this? What do you think, Jesus? She's guilty, so just say the word, and we'll make sure she pays the price.

"They kept demanding an answer, so he stood up again and said, 'All right, but let the one who has never sinned throw the first stone!'" John 8:7 (NLT)

You could have heard a pin drop.

Jesus then kneels again and continues to draw in the dirt, maybe recording their sins or recounting the laws of the Torah.

No one can be certain, but Jesus has spoken, leaving everyone speechless.

Mouths hang open. The crowd, suddenly silenced, stands in a circle, blinking, as if it would help make sense of what Jesus has just said. Some stammer to make a rebuttal but immediately go silent. Dumbfounded, their minds race to come up with another angle, another jab, another way to make this all go their way. No one could speak.

Now, *they* were in a trap.

If they pulled their arms back with the rocks in their palms, poised to stone her, they would be declaring that they had never sinned. If they didn't stone her for her sin, they would be guilty of not upholding the law.

Realizing the fragility of this predicament, the oldest Pharisees and scribes leave first, taking their own stones with them, knowing all too well the reality of their sin.

One by one, they leave. Soon, there is no one left to accuse her. No one is left holding stones.

There would be no execution today.

Only Jesus remains with the woman, and His full attention is on her. Jesus is positioned to settle the matter once and for all.

This time, the light touch on her arm is His, and is gentle and kind.

"'Where are your accusers? Didn't even one of them condemn you?'" John 8:10 (NLT)

She chokes back sobs and, with a dusty tear-stained face,

looks down at the earth from which she was created and back to her Creator.

"'No, Lord,' she said."

With the echo of stones being dropped one by one still in the woman's ears, Jesus tenderly says,

"'Neither do I. Go and sin no more.'" John 8:11 (NLT)

This is gentleness.

Gentleness can be displayed as a sensitivity to others or to ourselves. It also utilizes the other fruit, particularly kindness, patience, and peace, to do so. (Remember, the order of the fruit listed in Galatians matters. Every fruit of the Spirit builds on one another. Gentleness is no different.)

As we acknowledge the gentleness of Jesus, I do find it interesting the amount of movement recorded in this story:

- Jesus sits to teach.
- Apparently, he stands up when she approaches because He then stoops to write in the dirt.
- He then stands to address the Pharisees and stoops again.
- Finally, He stands to address the woman.

That's a lot of intentional motion within one story, and again, I believe this detail in John's account is important. Jesus is always intentional in what He does, and while I don't pretend to know His purpose here, what I do know is that when He addressed the Pharisees and the woman, He was standing. This conversation is serious to Him; it's life and death.

He was standing up to address sin.

Let's be clear. Jesus didn't go easy on the woman's sin. He didn't say, "It's okay. Adultery isn't a big deal; everyone is doing it, so I'll help you get out of it." No. She knows, *and He knows* that she was caught in sin, and the punishment is death. However, in gentleness, He gives her an opportunity to turn her life around.

In an interesting turn of events, Jesus also shows gentleness to the Pharisees. He could have put all their sin on display, and again, who knows, perhaps that's what He was writing in the dirt, but He gives them a way out. Just as He did with the woman, He gives *them* an opportunity to turn their lives around.

> The Eternal is gracious. He shows mercy to His people. For Him anger does not come easily, but faithful love does—and it is rich and abundant. But the Eternal's goodness is not exclusive—it is offered freely to all. His mercy extends to all His creation. Psalm 145:8-9 (VOICE)

Jesus is so gentle.

I need a gentle Jesus, too. When my sin is glaring and leaves scars on other people, I need to know that the same Jesus, who, in tenderness, looked at the woman's sin and declared "no condemnation," declares the same for me.

"There is therefore now no condemnation for those who are in

Christ Jesus. For the law of the Spirit of life has set you free in Christ Jesus from the law of sin and death." Romans 8:1–2 (ESV)

To be clear, the Lord doesn't wink at sin and never turns a blind eye to our actions. He disciplines us in love and for our good. I'm just so grateful that when He does, He does so in a way that doesn't ever shame us. That is gentleness.

As the woman left the circle that day and stepped over the pile of stones meant for her, I'm sure she was completely changed. (You cannot have an encounter with Jesus and not be.) She had been brought guilty to a circle of death and was sent away as someone set free to live. I'm sure she lived that out well.

Once you've experienced the gentleness of God, it marks you, especially when you know what you've done and what you deserve.

When you are more aware of your own sin and need for a Savior, it also helps you to be more willing to extend gentleness to others.

Gentleness can be a soft word. Gentleness can be tender understanding when you need it. And sometimes gentleness can be the sound of stones meant for you, hitting the ground.

PART 02: FINDING THE FRUIT OF GENTLENESS IN THE WORLD
-Tongue and Tone-

A GENTLE ANSWER DEFLECTS ANGER, BUT HARSH WORDS MAKE TEMPERS FLARE. —PROVERBS 15:1 (NLT)

It's not so much what you say but how you say it.

I've heard this statement and used it for years. Depending on how we say something, it can be interpreted in different ways, some not even close to how we intended.

A classic example heard in my house: "Where's my phone charger?"

If I say this in an inquisitive manner, quietly, almost talking to myself, it's benign. I'm simply walking around looking for my phone charger. On the other hand, if I'm running around the house frantically, holding a dead phone and see another human, specifically the 17-year-old male child I made, and I say the same sentence loudly in exasperation in his direction, well, it takes on quite a different meaning. (Admittedly, he's so much better than he used to be about taking my phone charger without asking. Love you, BJB.).

"Your tongue has the power of life and death. Those who love to talk will eat the fruit of their words." Proverbs 18:21 (NIRV)

Although I'm pretty reserved and much more prone to write

words than speak them, I do know that when I do open my mouth, I can either bless or bomb the room I'm in. It's a choice.

If I'm going to eat the fruit of my words—good or bad fruit—I need to be actively thinking before I open my mouth. The words I say AND how I say them matter.

My friend, Brandon, taught me the concept of "see it, say it." If I see something extraordinary in someone, or something rad that they've done, it's my spiritual responsibility to open my mouth and encourage them! This goes for total strangers as well as people I know and love. It displays the gentle love of Jesus to them. Alternatively, this concept is never, in any way, to be used as a weapon to "call it like I see it." (Remember, bless, not bomb...fruit of gentleness.)

This is such an important topic, especially in today's world, where people have seemingly lost the ability to tame their tongues or say things respectfully on social media and in public forums. Yes, in America, we have freedom of speech, praise the Lord, and we should speak up for injustice, the marginalized, and those who are persecuted for the sake of the Gospel, but that does not entitle us to use that freedom to harm others. Freedom of speech was made for just that—to *liberate people,* encourage them, and use our words for good. The vocabulary God created for us to use was never intended to criticize, slander, and cut down others from behind the safety of a computer screen.

Strong words, I know. But that's the point.

This is so important that the Bible dedicates an entire chapter in the book of James to taming the tongue: James chapter 3. Go ahead, go read it; I'll wait.

James warns us that our tongue can be like a bit in a horse's mouth or a rudder on a ship, small but mighty. He also compares the tongue to a fire and being full of poison.

Again, those are strong words, James!

Over 120 scripture passages are dedicated to using our tongues and words wisely. Most of those, I've found, are related to how the tongue can get us in trouble. (Another indicator that we get this more wrong than right).

Sometimes, we aren't aware of what our tone is conveying. We think we've communicated one thing, but instead, we communicated something entirely different, perhaps hurtful. (Anyone have a testimony of a text message gone wrong, where the tone is tough to read?) Or, I'm sure you've had moments in your life, like me, where you said something, and you immediately saw the effects of what you've said on the person's face. Something you said struck a nerve, whether you meant it to or not. Those are the moments when we need to respond in humility and use that same tongue to bring words of healing.

"Some people like to make cutting remarks, but the words of the wise soothe and heal." Proverbs 12:18 (TLB)

"I'm sorry, I was wrong" goes a long way. These words are where the fruit of gentleness can be on full display.

If, as believers, we are known by the way we love, and the primary way we do that is through communication, we are either sharing a reflection of Jesus through those words or, well, we're not.

It begs the question, how do we want to be known? Do you want to be characterized as someone who uses their mouth to be quick to bless the Lord, talk about what He's done in your life, and encourage others? Or, will you be characterized by cynicism, bitterness, and an I-must-have-the-last-word attitude?

"Let the words of my mouth and the meditation of my heart be acceptable in your sight, O Lord, my rock and my redeemer." Psalm 19:14 (ESV)

May we each use words that bless and heal and reveal the fruit of gentleness to others. Let's commit to choosing our words carefully and allowing what we say to show a world that so desperately needs hope, the gentle love of the Father.

-Training Wheels-

LORD, SHOW ME YOUR WAYS. TEACH ME HOW TO
FOLLOW YOU. GUIDE ME IN YOUR TRUTH. TEACH
ME. YOU ARE GOD MY SAVIOR. I PUT MY HOPE
IN YOU ALL DAY LONG. —PSALM 25:4-5 (NIRV)

By nature, I like learning new things, how things work, and how to make things better. This doesn't mean that I'm good at everything I learn about or try to do, but I enjoy the process nonetheless.

While my creativity leans more toward the analytical rather than artistic, I try to flex my other creative muscles every now and then. Recently, I saw something that inspired me. A company was selling a detailed paint-by-number kit to recreate a painting of plumerias. By now, you know how I feel about plumerias. I couldn't press "buy now" fast enough! I'm not a painter, (and, truth be told, painting completely intimidates me), but for some reason, this felt safe. Elementary, but safe.

I have watched other friends, like my friend Carrie, paint and create art, and it seems effortless to her. She knows how to hold the brushes and apply the proper pressure, how much water to use, and how to mix the colors to achieve what she envisions. On the other hand, I look at a blank canvas, and it's *paralyzing*. I think, what if I mess it up? What if I mix all the colors together and it just turns into a blob of brown? What if I start well but get halfway done and somehow can't figure out how to finish?

Needless to say, I needed a paint-by-number to learn how it

works. A paint-by-number to create a rudimentary version of what I see my friends who are professional artists do in their sleep. A paint-by-number to help me know the way.

I ordered the kit, and soon after it arrived, I set my sights on an upcoming free Saturday morning. I unpacked the box, found a spot on the front porch, and began my within-my-comfort-zone painting journey.

Paint-by-number is like an artist's version of training wheels. In the same way a child needs training wheels to learn how to ride a bike, we often need something or someone to show us the way to God's presence, to learn how to experience Him in the everyday, and to discover ways to grow in the fruit of the Spirit.

When I'm learning a new facet of the Lord's character or leaning into a lesson He wants to teach me, I realize I need to put on spiritual training wheels and borrow someone's faith until I am ready to do it or apply it on my own. Sometimes, it's hard to have faith to believe God's promises for something you're praying about or want to see Him do. This is where having a friend come alongside you in faith can be so important to gently encourage you in your journey. We're not meant to do life alone.

Some of you might be in a stage of growth where you might not need these types of spiritual training wheels; instead, you may have been experiencing God's presence and seeing fruit grow in your daily life for years. If that's you—amazing! Consider coming alongside those who could be encouraged by your experience. Pointing others to the ways you engage God's presence and live out the fruit of the Spirit in your daily life can inspire others and help them grow in their faith.

"So encourage each other and build each other up, just as you are already doing." 1 Thessalonians 5:11 (NLT)

Either way, this is gentleness in action.

Whenever we are learning a new skill, it's okay to come to the gentle realization that since we've never done this thing before, we can't expect ourselves to be experts the first time (or even the tenth). It's okay not to get it right. It's okay to ask for help. This goes for learning to paint, but it also applies to learning to grow in the fruit of the Spirit. This includes growing in the way we respond to others when we're learning to put those fruit-filled characteristics into action, and growing in our understanding of how to spur others on to grow as well.

Growing means things are changing. As things change, we have to remember to be gentle with ourselves in the process. We would never get mad at a child learning how to ride a bike with training wheels; we should not get frustrated with ourselves when we have spiritual training wheels on and are learning how to navigate life in a new way with the Lord.

Sometimes, we need to extend the fruit of gentleness to ourselves, too.

In the same way that I am learning this new artistic skill and am *slowly* getting better, I hope you are also learning to recognize His presence and the fruit of the Spirit in ordinary moments. Simply raising our awareness of His "with-ness" in our daily lives will help us develop this skill.

If you need your own set of "training wheels," don't worry or compare yourself to others' progress. Their journey to Jesus has no bearing on yours. The pursuit of the Lord and the get-up-and-try-again-even-if-you-aren't-sure-how way is all that matters. He loves you and is excited to share all His wonders with you. The Lord is gentle and kind and right there with you on your journey to becoming more like Him.

Let your gentleness
be evident to all.
The Lord is near.

Philippians 4:5 (NIV)

Chapter 09

self-control

SELF-CONTROL | KA PĀKIKO

What kind of fun day was our Creator having when he started working on the beautiful bird of paradise? The flower's colors, the shape, the nod to the avian world? It's spectacular! Everything about it screams, "go big or go home." But, when I learned that it takes the bird of paradise 3 to 6 years to produce its first bloom, it seemed to me almost as if it knows it needs to learn a thing or two before showing off. This reminded me of the fruit of self-control. It waits. It restrains its flashy, riotous flowers that scream *"Shazam!"* to simply grow leaves, multiply in size, and become stronger. Once it does bloom, it is finally large enough to support the magnificently prolific flowers.

It takes a humble attitude to display self-control, especially when a person knows what they are capable of. Jesus displayed extreme self-control when He came to earth on "Operation: Rescue Humanity." He is God, yet He came humbly robed as a child. There is no better example of magnificence under restraint than our beautiful King Jesus.

I have green eyes. My dad has green eyes. My mom has green eyes, and my sister has green eyes. Growing up, it never occurred to me that green eyes were rare since everyone close to me had them. (According to Google, only 2% of the world's population has green eyes—and 4 of those 2% are in my family.) That said, I've always loved the color green. Perhaps, it's because it's always staring at me in the mirror, or perhaps it reminds me of all these beautiful flowers and plants we've talked about for the last eight chapters. Regardless, I felt it was fitting to start this book with a fresh, bright green and to end it with this darker green that feels older, like seasoned growth. I hope that's what you have experienced as we've journeyed through the fruit of the Spirit together.

...for God gave us
a spirit not of fear
but of power and
love and self-
control.

2 Timothy 1:7 (ESV)

self-control

A person without self-control is like a city with broken-down walls.

Proverbs 25:28 (NLT)

PART 01: FINDING THE FRUIT OF SELF-CONTROL IN THE WORD OF GOD
-Jesus On The Cross-

WHEN HE APPEARED IN HUMAN FORM, HE HUMBLED HIMSELF IN OBEDIENCE TO GOD AND DIED A CRIMINAL'S DEATH ON A CROSS. —PHILIPPIANS 2:7B-8 (NLT)

The man hanging on the cross was barely alive, barely recognizable as a human. His face was black and blue, and His hands and feet were torn wide open. Fighting for breath and with a body full of gaping wounds, He was not only covered in blood, but it ran down the cross and pooled beneath Him.

Although horrible to look at, those gathered could not help but stare. Some gawked in approval. Others gasped in disbelief. *How could this be happening?*

A sign had been placed above His head: "King of the Jews."

We will never know, this side of eternity, the full gravity of what Jesus felt in those moments. Yes, there was physical pain beyond human words; it was beyond brutal. But the pain of being separated from His father while having every sin placed on Him was what was killing Him.

During those hours on the cross, Jesus showed us the most significant measure of self-control ever displayed.

Being fully God while fully man, He could have stopped the entire proceeding at any moment. He could have called down any number of ministering angels to make the pain less horrific. He could have pulled off some sort of miraculous now-you-see-me-now-you-don't kind of moment and simply disappeared off the cross. He could have healed His own wounds.

He did not.

He chose the cross and every aspect of a public, humiliating, agonizing, unthinkable death. He chose the pain. He chose to suffer, and worst of all, even though He was sinless (1 John 3:5), He chose to have the sin of the world placed upon Himself as the perfect, holy sacrifice, once and for all. It was the only way for "Operation: Rescue Humanity" to be successful.

> For God sent Christ Jesus to take the punishment for our sins and to end all God's anger against us. He used Christ's blood and our faith as the means of saving us from his wrath. Romans 3:25a (TLB)

Sin requires a blood sacrifice for atonement. This has been clear and set up since the Garden of Eden. Adam and Eve sinned, and to make amends for their sin and cover their nakedness, God had to kill an animal to give them hides to wear. Blood had to be shed.

Fast-forward several thousand years, and we see God establish a blood-sacrifice system in Exodus to restore the broken relationship between God and humanity.

Throughout Old Testament history, we see humanity striving in every way possible to make amends with God. But nothing they do or anything they try to repair their separation from God is ever close to enough.

Then, in a way that truly characterizes the upside-down Kingdom that Jesus taught about, we see Him perfectly and completely making amends for sin once and for all to make up for all the ways humanity failed to do so.

Wild.

> We are sure of this because Christ was raised from the dead, and he will never die again. Death no longer has any power over him. When he died, he died once to break the power of sin. But now that he lives, he lives for the glory of God. So you also should consider yourselves to be dead to the power of sin and alive to God through Christ Jesus.
> Romans 6:9-11 (NLT)

This means you and I can now boldly approach the throne of grace (Hebrews 4:16) and share eternity with Him (John 3:16). There is no greater news in all the world!

The first blood sacrifice ever made was made by God. The last blood sacrifice ever needed was made by Jesus. A complete work. First and last.

When Jesus submitted to death on the cross, the self-control He displayed to follow through with "Operation: Rescue Humanity" was the culmination of a life lived in accordance with the Spirit.

What started as a life motivated by love, joy, and peace, displayed in patience, kindness, goodness, gentleness and faithfulness, was anchored by self-control. It was the last piece needed to complete the mission He set out to do.

While still fully God, He willingly laid that aside and with the ultimate act of self-control, stepped into human skin. Out of love, He offered His life as a ransom for many. (Mark 10:45) He became the visible expression of God's love for the world and set before us the example by which to live our lives.

Majesty under restraint.

As followers of Jesus, self-control is both something that can naturally grow in us and a discipline that must be developed. The more we spend time with the Lord and desire to be like Him, the more this fruit will naturally be evident in our lives. In addition, self-control, like the other characteristics of a life fueled by and patterned after God's Spirit, requires determined discipline and difficult choices to live out.

We see all of this in the life of Jesus.

Jesus didn't choose the easy way out. He did not choose what He wanted, but what the Father wanted to do through Him (Luke 22:42).

May we all be willing to grow and develop self-control so that we can embody all the characteristics of a life formed by the Spirit that will make us more like Him.

PART 02: FINDING THE FRUIT OF SELF-CONTROL IN THE WORLD
-Fold Your Hands-

A PERSON WITHOUT SELF-CONTROL IS LIKE A CITY
WITH BROKEN-DOWN WALLS. —PROVERBS 25:28 (NLT)

Man, oh, man. Sometimes I just get so mad.

When I sense that I have been wronged—or worse, someone I love has—look out, world. Mama Bear has entered the chat.

I can feel it creeping up my neck, and my blood pressure starts to rise. I'm known to be pretty expressive anyway and also known to talk (and sing) with my hands. (I am actually not sure if I can have a conversation without talking with my hands.) So, when I'm mad, this demonstrative use of my hands to explain whatever I'm feeling goes into overdrive. Never violent, but wow, I can sure wave my arms around like crazy to make my point. Can you relate?

When I am mad, it usually appears in two forms: the ultra-quiet or the ultra-explosive. There is no in-between. I'm not proud of it, but I am human. I may be small, but I can be pretty spicy. After all, dynamite does come in small packages.

When our boys were toddlers, and before they could fully communicate, they would cry or use their bodies to relay their frustration. Sometimes, it was because a friend took away a toy. Sometimes, it was a lack of understanding why mom or dad would make them eat something healthy (we are terrible parents), or sometimes, it would simply be their inability to communicate with their limited vocabulary. Each scenario caused outbursts; each needed training to help them grow into children, and later, adults who could manage their emotions appropriately.

As parents, we knew that in these toddler years, outbursts were to be expected. We also knew that as adults with working vocabularies and life experiences that had taught us to regulate our emotions, we could help our boys. We wanted to give them tools to help them appropriately express frustration and anger. Still, we didn't know everything about raising children, so we took parenting classes to equip ourselves for each age and stage of their growth and development. Eventually, we even wound up teaching those classes. This didn't make us experts (and still doesn't), but we were given a valuable teaching tool that we successfully used and passed along to other parents.

Fold your hands.

Expressing emotion in a healthy way is essential for mental and emotional health. However, when you are two years old and don't have the same emotional capacity, life experience, frame of reference, or vocabulary as a 35-year-old, you need to learn to handle life's little frustrations (like the broccoli touching the peaches) in an age-appropriate way.

When the frustrated-toddler emotions started to rise, we would have our boys take a deep breath, clasp their hands together, fingers interlocking, and calmly tell them, "Little Fella, fold your hands and get self-control. Then, I can help you with (whatever you're frustrated about)."

Within 5-10 seconds, the crying would stop, their breathing would be under control, and the angry energy that needed somewhere to go would be directed to those little hands folded together. It was kind of magic.

In times of non-conflict, i.e., not in the middle of a meltdown, we would teach them principles about self-control from the Bible. From an early age, we would have them memorize scriptures like Proverbs 25:28. We made up little hand motions and would laugh together about not wanting to be like a city with broken-down walls. *No! We want to be a stronnnng city!* (Imagine precious little toddler muscle motions.)

(Sidebar: Parents teaching children the Word of God is a joy and memorizing it never returns void.)

One afternoon, I was walking around my local Walmart with my then-3-year-old, Ethan. He was seated calmly in the cart, and while I can't remember the scenario exactly, I remember I got pretty frustrated while in the store. Maybe it was at a cashier; maybe it was because they were out of something, or maybe just maybe I was exhausted, and doing my best to be a mom and work a full-time job and keep it all together. Regardless, I lost my cool and started very expressively using my hands to explain my frustration.

In an embarrassingly big voice that only a 3-year-old can use in public situations, Ethan said, "Mommy, you need to fold your hands and get self-control!"

He was right. And so, I did. I took a deep breath, folded my hands, and right there in Walmart, my toddler gave me a tool to help me not have broken down walls in my life.

Broken walls that would allow anger to have a foothold.

Walls that, if broken, would allow the enemy to steal my joy.

Broken walls that, if left unattended, would allow all kinds of unhealthy emotions to take root in my life and family.

This practice of "folding your hands" is still alive and well in the Banks family, even though my boys are grown. My husband and I still use it to this day. Not long ago, I recently heard my husband on the phone having a difficult conversation. I watched him set the phone down, put it on speaker, take a deep breath, and fold his hands. We gave each other a knowing smile before he picked the phone back up and continued. I think it's pretty safe to say we all are a work in progress and that we all need to continue to grow in the fruit of self-control. It's the final fruit listed in Galatians 5:22-23 but should not be overlooked in any way. Using it is necessary to handle life's most frustrating situations appropriately and is essential for not destroying a relationship in anger (and for not getting yourself kicked out of Walmart). It's not just for toddlers; self-control is for you and me, too.

-See Green-

OPEN MY EYES TO SEE THE MIRACLES IN
YOUR TEACHINGS. —PSALM 119:18 (NCV)

Although it was a stormy day, my friend Dana and I headed down a muddy road in a four-wheel-drive Jeep to reach a tiny section of rocky beach. It was not known for its location or even the view—we were there for something else: trash that had washed ashore.

Many years ago, before strict environmental laws and regulations existed, there was an industrial offshore dumping ground near this beach, full of glass and ceramic tile. Over multiple decades, this waste has been violently tossed, sanded, and smoothed by the sea. Today, pieces wash up on the shore as beautifully tumbled sea glass. On any given day, you can walk the tiny section of rocky beach and find clear, green, brown, and even blue sea glass and broken tile. It's like a treasure hunt—and always a place I hear the Lord speak.

On this particular day, we didn't go in with high hopes for finding many treasures because it was high tide and stormy, and the beach would be mostly covered by water.

And it was just as we expected. The surf was pounding, and the beach was barely exposed. We threw caution to the wind and decided to search for sea-treasures anyway.

Dana headed off to the right, and I went left. I decided, if I was there, my hunt would be purposeful. I would only look for green glass. Stooping down, I looked closely at the sand, and said out loud, "See green."

I was telling my brain to block out all the black rocks, broken pieces of brown bottles, seashells, and random pieces of actual trash and only see the green glass pieces. Slowly, my eyes began to home in on the slivers of green hidden amongst all the other sea-tumbled pieces. After 10-15 minutes of hunting, I was holding several lovely pieces of green sea glass.

Right about that time, Dana walked over and showed me her multi-colored treasures and mentioned she wished she had found more blue sea glass.

"Try this," I told her. "Look right here in this pile of sand and just see blue. Once you train your eyes to see it, you can't unsee it. It's not as if the blue suddenly appears; it's been there all along, but sometimes we just have to train our eyes to see it."

Often, we miss what is right in front of us. We are blind to what the Lord is doing in our lives, and we don't see the good in people or our circumstances. Sometimes, we miss blessings that are in the middle of our path because they're disguised as the unexpected, like beautiful sea glass amongst all the rocks and sand on a day where there should have been none. The good things are there; we just need the self-control to focus on them.

Sometimes, we need a friend to encourage us to be more aware of what is right in front of us. This was true of Elisha and his servant in 2 Kings 6. A vast army surrounded them, and for all practical purposes, what they could see meant certain defeat. Elisha, however, knew God and knew what He could do. He had faith that the Lord was with them and knew that if his servant *could just see it,* his faith would rise, and he would not be afraid.

> Then Elisha prayed, "Lord, open his eyes and let him see!" And the Lord opened the young man's eyes so that he could see horses of fire and chariots of fire everywhere upon the mountain! 2 Kings 6:17 (TLB)

We need to purposefully position godly mentors, friends, and people of faith in our lives who will help us to see what we cannot see, to believe for what we cannot believe, and to have the self-control to train our eyes to focus on the Lord, not the swirling circumstances around us.

> I ask—ask the God of our Master, Jesus Christ, the God of glory—to make you intelligent and discerning in knowing him personally, your eyes focused and clear, so that you can see exactly what it is he is calling you to do, grasp the immensity of this glorious way of life he has for his followers, oh, the utter extravagance of his work in us who trust him—endless energy, boundless strength! Ephesians 1:18 (MSG)

Dana left the beach that day with a handful of beautiful blue sea glass. But the Lord spoke to us both during that purposeful treasure hunt on the beach. We learned to train our eyes to see the beauty right in front of us—to have the self-control not to be distracted by the rest, but to truly fix our eyes on everything He wanted to show us.

As we grow in self-control, we will learn to focus the eyes of our understanding so we accurately see the truth and blessings that exist. Let's always be found searching for the treasures that the

Lord has right before our eyes, no matter the circumstances, and thank Him for that fruit-filled perspective every single day.

CONCLUSION

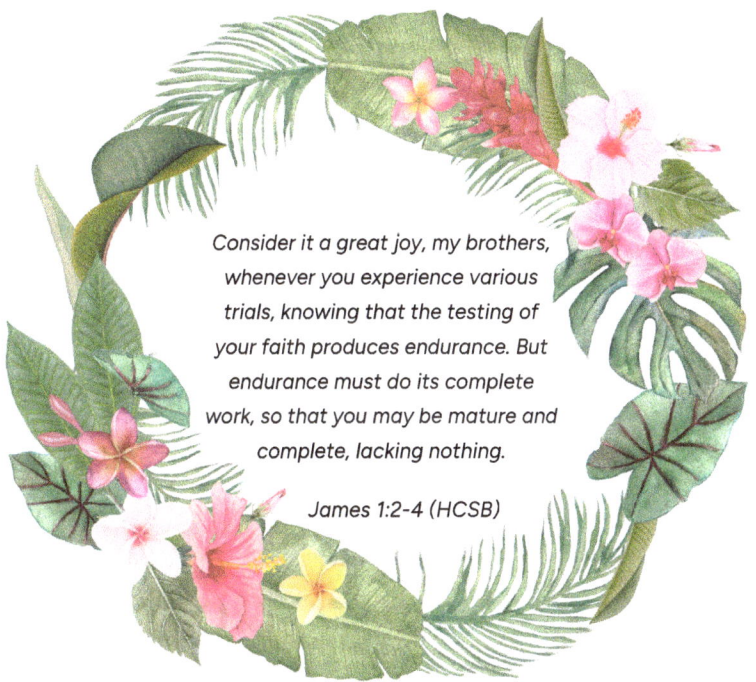

Consider it a great joy, my brothers, whenever you experience various trials, knowing that the testing of your faith produces endurance. But endurance must do its complete work, so that you may be mature and complete, lacking nothing.

James 1:2-4 (HCSB)

With our eyes wide open to God's presence, we can find the fruit of the Spirit all around us. Whether in the sound of a friend's voice, a coffee done just right, a worship song that speaks right to your heart, or in God's nearness at a time when you need Him most.

But—what happens when you're struggling with your circumstances and the fruit of the Spirit in your life seems more withered than wonderful? What happens when you can't find everyday fruit?

Enter James.

James basically opens his epistle with, "Hello all. My name is James. Life is going to be hard."

I'm not sure if this is an excellent letter-writing technique to draw in the reader or just a solid wake-up call, but either way, James doesn't mess around with the truth.

I agree that James' statement that we should be filled with joy when faced with hard things is hard to swallow. That is not often my first response. However, it should be a clue to me that with the proper perspective, joy (along with the other fruit) can be found just around the corner if I'm willing to let the time of testing do its full work so that I "may be mature and complete, lacking nothing." (James 1:4)

To be clear, here's what James is not saying: he is not saying when trials come, you should be happy about it and act as if everything is totally fine.

He *is* saying that when trials come, they should act as a reminder. While life will be hard, and none of us are exempt from it (see John 16:33), those hard things are an opportunity to grow in our faith and Christ-likeness, which is our entire goal. The goal is not to tiptoe through life without trial; the goal is to endure the trials in a way and to a degree that the trial refines and shapes us to look a little bit more like Jesus on the other side.

That's growing a fruit-filled life.

For any fruit of the Spirit to grow in us, we often must walk through times of testing so that we also develop the partner characteristic, or fruit-friend, endurance. Endurance, or the ability to continue to do difficult things for an extended period of time, is just that. It makes the other fruit, like patience and self-control, grow all the more beautiful.

"Do not forget to rejoice, for hope is always just around the corner. Hold up through the hard times that are coming, and devote yourselves to prayer." Romans 12:12 (VOICE)

If you have faced something difficult and persevered, you may feel a sense of deep satisfaction, dare I say, *joy*, knowing that you've endured that trial or hardship!

If you are in a hard season, I've been there. If you are knee-deep in something that feels neck-deep, I see you. If you are struggling to find what the fruit of the Spirit looks like in the middle of your challenge, I understand. Best of all, the Lord does, too, and has not abandoned you in the middle of it. These challenges are refining us, making us better, and can draw us closer to Jesus if we allow them to. Be encouraged that you are developing a testimony of faith that will be the evidence of the Lord's work in your life—the fruit of the Spirit on display.

Throughout the book, we've seen examples of how these characteristics have been lived out in scripture, how to live out those characteristics as representatives of God's people, and how to discover them in everyday moments.

As we've grown in fruit-finding, we've also learned about many different types of Hawaiian flowers. On the last page of every chapter, you may have noticed a tropical bouquet growing in size. (If you didn't, go peek—they are so beautiful!) Chapter by chapter, we've added one flower representing a fruit of the Spirit to the bouquet. Now, we've brought together all nine. This bouquet is an image of what the life of a Spirit-filled believer in Jesus can look like.

The fruit of the Spirit are tied together, complementing one another in ways that make our lives as vibrant and fragrant as an armload of Hawaiian tropical flowers. Alone, any fruit of the Spirit is admirable and beautiful, but together, the beauty becomes unmatched! Let's consciously try to gather into a bouquet the fruit of the Spirit in our own lives and become a sweet fragrance to those around us as we spend time with and learn from Jesus.

It's time to take a final look back at the key verse for this book, Galatians 5:22-23 (ESV).

"But the fruit of the Spirit is love, joy, peace, patience, kindness, goodness, faithfulness, gentleness, self-control; against such things there is no law."

Jesus is perfect and fully embodies every fruit of the Spirit. There never has, nor will there ever be, a greater display of:

Love

"For this is how God loved the world: he gave his one and only Son, so that everyone who believes in him will not perish but have eternal life." John 3:16 (NLT)

Joy

We do this by keeping our eyes on Jesus, the champion who initiates and perfects our faith. Because of the joy awaiting him, he endured the cross, disregarding its shame. Now he is seated in the place of honor beside God's throne. Hebrews 12:2 (NLT)

Peace

But now in Christ Jesus you who once were far off have been brought near by the blood of Christ. For he himself is our peace... Ephesians 2:13-14a (ESV)

Patience

The Lord is not slow in keeping his promise, as some understand slowness. Instead he is patient with you, not wanting anyone to perish, but everyone to come to repentance. 2 Peter 3:9 (NIV)

Kindness

But then something happened: God our Savior and His overpowering love and kindness for humankind entered our world; He came to save us. It's not that we earned it by doing good works or righteous deeds; He came because He is merciful. Titus 3:4-5a (VOICE)

Goodness

The Lord is good to all, and his mercy is over all that he has made. Psalm 145:9 (ESV)

Faithfulness

And when he was living as a man, he humbled himself and was fully obedient to God, even when that caused his death—death on a cross. Philippians 2:8 (NCV)

Gentleness

"Put My yoke upon your shoulders—it might appear heavy at first, but it is perfectly fitted to your curves. Learn from Me, for I am gentle and humble of heart. When you are yoked to Me, your weary souls will find rest." Matthew 11:29 (VOICE)

And Self-Control

He who did not spare his own Son, but gave him up for us all—how will he not also, along with him, graciously give us all things? Romans 8:32 (NIV)

He is THE model of what it looks like to surrender our lives to the Father completely, and also what it looks like to let that relationship mark us so much that we naturally bear fruit and help bring it out in others.

I know we are not Jesus, and that we will not do everything by His example, even as much as we'd like. However, every day that we choose to love the way He does, learn to see examples of the fruit of the Spirit in His creation, or perhaps work to emulate His characteristics, we are, little by little, becoming more like Him. As you know by now, the fruit of the Spirit doesn't just happen by chance in our lives. It's our responsibility to nurture and tend to its growth and then go live it out.

Since this is the kind of life we have chosen, the life of the Spirit, let us make sure that we do not just hold it as an idea in our heads or a sentiment in our hearts, but work out its implications in every detail of our lives. Galatians 5:25 (MSG)

So, as we grow, may we all be able to identify more love, joy, peace, and patience in ourselves and the world around us, be characterized by more kindness, goodness, faithfulness, and gentleness, and become more self-controlled. May we discover and develop a life formed by the fruit of the Spirit, and may we be found finding everyday fruit.

The bouquet of your life is going to be beautiful; I just know it.

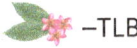 —TLB

ACKNOWLEDGMENTS

To King Jesus, the Maker of the Flowers: Every word of this is for you. Thank you for letting me use my little words to try to tell the world what you mean to me and for giving me the opportunity to taste and see how good you are in everyday moments.

To My Three Boys: If I have any good fruit in me, you've helped develop it. I could not love you more. You are so rad.

To Lydia Jane: You've been my #1 sidekick for this whole project. What a joy to do this with you. For the vision you've carried, the florals you designed, the social media you managed, and the way your life shows the fruit of a life connected to Jesus so beautifully—thank you.

To Marney: Once again, you've taken this little dream and helped me explain it in a way that was so much better than draft one. Thank you for your editing-ninja skills and faithful friendship.

To Typewriter Creative Co: I couldn't imagine trusting this book to anyone but you, and I am grateful to have you as my partner in publishing again. You brought life to the fruit and the flowers when I wasn't sure they would see the light of day. Thank you for carrying the vision in my heart all the way to print with such grace and professionalism.

To Adam and Dana: Thank you for being true friends when we needed you most. Sometimes, the Lord reveals the best things at just the right time. Your friendship is fruit in due season.

To the Wait-ers: Your dedication and support, from the Wonder to the Fruit, have been instrumental in my writing work and to the community we're building. I'm deeply grateful for each of you and the joy you bring to my life. Thank you.

LEARN HAWAIIAN

"The two official languages of Hawai'i are *'Olelo Hawaii* (Hawaiian) and English. The Hawaiian language is a Polynesian dialect with only 13 letters in its alphabet: A, E, H, I, K, L, M, N, O, P, U, W, and the *'okina* (*'*). The *'okina* is a glottal stop, like the sound between the oh's in oh-oh, and is a consonant. The *'okina* and *kahakō* (*-*), or macron over a vowel, change the pronunciation and meaning of a word.

The Hawaiian language has 18 sounds:

\a\ - like "ah" in "above"
\ā\ - like "aah" in "far"
\e\ - like "eh" in "bet"
\ē\ - like "ay" in "pay"
\i\ - like "y" as in "city"
\ī\ - like "ee" in "see"
\o\ - like "oh" in "low"
\ō\ - like "oh" in "sole"
\u\ - like "oo" in "hoot"
\ū\ - like "oo" in "moon"
Plus, \he\, \ke\, \la\, \mu\, \nu\, \pi\, \we\, and W with a \v\sound.

Some vowels are diphthongs, forming a single sound as in \ai\ in Waimea. In general, the consonants are pronounced as in English with the exception of W. W can be either a \v\ or a \w\ sound."[7]*

* Mahalo to Gina Chun from The Hawai'i Visitors and Convention Bureau, who granted me very special permission to use this Hawaiian language description in my book.

NOW YOU TRY!

Galatians 5:22-23 in Hawaiian (KBH)

"Akā, ʻo ka hua na ka ʻUhane, ʻo ia ke aloha, ka ʻoliʻoli, ke kuʻikahi, ke ahonui, ka lokomaikaʻi, ka maikaʻi, ka manaʻoʻiʻo, ke akahai, ka pākiko; ʻaʻohe kānāwai pāpā mai ia mau mea."

Translation:

Akā, - but
ʻo ka hua - the fruit
na ka ʻUhane, - by the Spirit
ʻo ia - is
ke aloha, - love
ka ʻoliʻoli, - joy
ke kuʻikahi, - agreement (peace)
ke ahonui, - patience
ka lokomaikaʻi, - kindness (literally means "inner goodness")
ka maikaʻi, - the best (goodness)
ka manaʻoʻiʻo, - faith
ke akahai, - gentleness
ka pākiko; - temperance (self-control)
ʻaʻohe - there is none
kānāwai - law
pāpā mai - prohibited, not
ia mau mea - those things

(Mahalo nui loa to Aunty Haunani Pacheco for generously recording Galatians 5:22-23 in Hawaiian for me while in Kauai in 2024. Scan the QR code to listen to her beautiful version.)

THE MEANING OF "ALOHA"

The Hawaiian greeting *"Aloha"* is popular and might be, before reading this book, all you've ever known about the Hawaiian Islands. But in Hawaiian culture, this little word carries much more meaning than simply a greeting or something you'd see on a souvenir mug. To the Hawaiian people, and according to Hawaii.edu,

> These are traits of character that express the charm, warmth and sincerity of Hawaii's people. It was the working philosophy of native Hawaiians and was presented as a gift to the people of Hawai'i. "Aloha" means mutual regard and affection and extends warmth in caring with no obligation in return. "Aloha" is the essence of relationships in which each person is important to every other person for collective existence. "Aloha" means to hear what is not said, to see what cannot be seen and to know the unknowable.

Not only does "Aloha" itself translate to "love," but it can also be explained in an acronym:

"**A**kahai", meaning kindness to be expressed with tenderness;
"**L**ōkahi", meaning unity, to be expressed with harmony;
"'**O**lu'olu" meaning agreeable, to be expressed with pleasantness;
"**H**a'aha'a", meaning humility, to be expressed with modesty;
"**A**honui", meaning patience, to be expressed with perseverance[8]

Did you see it? So many fruits of a Spirit-filled life are woven right into the fabric of the meaning of the word "Aloha." It's been there all along! So when you give the greeting "Aloha" to someone, it's not just something you say because you've been to the islands; you are actually speaking over them a blessing to be filled with all the fruit of the Spirit.

So to you, *Aloha*, my friend.
Aloha.

NOTES

LOVE:

1. Ingrid Goff-Maidoff, "God Spoke Today In Flowers." *What Holds Us: New and Selected Poems*. (Chilmark, MA: Sarah's Circle Publishing, 2011).

2. "Love the Lord your God with all your heart and with all your soul and with all your mind. This is the first and greatest commandment. And the second is like it: Love your neighbor as yourself. All the Law and the Prophets hang on these two commandments." Matthew 22:37-40 (NIV)

3. Psalm 139:16, Luke 12:7, Psalm 56:8, Psalm 33:13, Hebrews 8:12, Genesis 16:13.

JOY:

4. Lewis, C. S. 2014. "The Lion, the Witch and the Wardrobe." epubbooks. epubbooks.com.

5. Hebrews 12:2

PATIENCE:

6. Turnage, Marc. 2016. AG News. https://news.ag.org/en/article-repository/news/2016/05/sometimes-a-rooster-is-not-a-rooster.

LEARN HAWAIIAN:

7. Hawai'i Visitors and Convention Bureau. 2024. *The Language of Hawai'i,* Experience Kaua'i. Winter-Spring ed. Kahului, HI: Pacific Media Group.

THE MEANING OF "ALOHA":

8. Center for Labor Education and Research, "The Law of the Aloha Spirit," Hawaii.edu, University of Hawai'i System, Accessed September 14, 2024. https://www.hawaii.edu/uhwo/clear/home/lawaloha.html.

ABOUT THE AUTHOR

After writing in secret for 15 years, Tara L. Banks felt prompted to develop her work into a book. The very next day, she accidentally lost every word she'd ever written. Refusing to give up, she realized that God was guiding her to write about the lessons she needed to learn through moments like that one. From that experience, her debut book, *Waiting On Wonders,* was born.

When she's not writing, Tara can be found sharing her experiences through speaking and coaching worship teams, having served for over 20 years as a Worship Pastor at Seacoast Church in Charleston, South Carolina. She's married to her college sweetheart, Greg, and they have two sons-of-thunder, Ethan and Brody, plus a daughter-in-love, Lydia. When she's not tinkering with her '73 CJ-5 Jeep or dreaming of Hawaii, you will likely find her waiting on wonders and searching for the fruit of the Spirit in everyday life. Learn more at TaraLBanks.com.

READ MORE FROM
TARA L. BANKS

Waiting On Wonders is a 40-day devotional focused on experiencing God's presence in everyday moments. It is available through all major online bookstores. Additionally, you can find a signed special edition of the book and other merch exclusively at TaraLBanks.com.

Tara also regularly writes on Substack at TaraLBanks.substack.com and on Instagram @taraLbanks.

TaraLBanks.com